# LIFEBOAT

## Also by Maggie Craddock

*The Authentic Career: Following the Path of Self-Discovery to Professional Fulfillment* (New World Library, 2004)

*Power Genes: Understanding Your Power Persona — and How to Wield It at Work* (Harvard Business Review Press, 2011)

# LIFEBOAT

## NAVIGATING UNEXPECTED
## CAREER CHANGE AND DISRUPTION

## MAGGIE CRADDOCK

New World Library
Novato, California

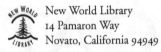
New World Library
14 Pamaron Way
Novato, California 94949

Text design by Tona Pearce Myers

Library of Congress Cataloging-in-Publication data is available.

First printing, May 2020

ISBN 978-1-60868-684-1
Ebook ISBN 978-1-60868-685-8

Printed in Canada on 100% postconsumer-waste recycled paper

New World Library is proud to be a Gold Certified Environmentally Responsible Publisher. Publisher certification awarded by Green Press Initiative. www.greenpressinitiative.org

10   9   8   7   6   5   4   3   2   1

*To my husband, best friend, and partner,*
*Charles Schneider,*
*whose presence makes the journey of life a source of infinite joy*

# CONTENTS

# Introduction

# THE LIFEBOAT PROCESS

We all like to think we are prepared for the unexpected. When it comes to our professional self-image, most of us strive to be adaptable, collaborative, and resilient. Yet in my work as an executive coach, I've listened to many people describe professional situations where they were caught off guard and discovered that their reactions under pressure surprised them.

Whether it's a thought leader who gets tongue-tied at a critical moment or a manager who loses his or her temper during a staff meeting, many people are bewildered by their own conduct when the stakes are high.

These eye-opening gaps between how people hope they will respond and how they actually react are symptomatic of a breakdown in trust. This may start as a breakdown in trust between organizations and their employees, but it can gradually evolve into a *breakdown in trust within individuals themselves.*

Here are just a few of the professional challenges people have shared with me and the questions these situations have prompted.

Circumstances such as these leave many hardworking people feeling emotionally paralyzed, tempted to make impulsive decisions, and striving to please external authority figures at precisely the moment they should be listening to their authentic inner voice:

- My boss just resigned unexpectedly: Who can I trust to help keep my career on track?
- Power struggles keep erupting at my firm: How do I handle my emotional reactions to dysfunctional behavior and protect my professional reputation?
- Earnings are down and our firm needs to run leaner: How do I convince my top talent to do hands-on work they had previously been delegating?
- Everyone in my department is under constant pressure: How do I find the inner strength to stay patient and present with my family while keeping up at work?

What do *you* do when unexpected problems arise that threaten to overwhelm you, undermine your ability to trust others, or even compromise your ability to align your personal and professional values? In this book, I offer a method for survival that I call the Lifeboat Process. This process will help you trust yourself under pressure, adapt as necessary, and take effective action to keep your job, life, relationships, and career afloat.

Stories help us unlock personal truths that we can't access when our minds are focused on routine responsibilities. The Lifeboat Process stems from lessons I have gathered from the *Titanic* and formalized into a process of exploration, discussion, and awareness. I have used this process to help clients leverage their resources in all kinds of unpredictable and even potentially catastrophic professional environments, whether they are entering the workforce, contemplating a job transition, seeking to become a more effective leader, or navigating a corporate or professional disaster.

This method uses the events of the *Titanic*'s sinking — and most particularly, how a group of strangers managed to survive together in Lifeboat #6 — to draw profound lessons for navigating the upheaval and difficult challenges in today's workplace. Using the real-life experiences of these maritime survivors, I have created a practical guide for spotting trouble, managing fear, trusting oneself, fostering cooperative and supportive teams, and taking simple yet effective action in any crisis. By mastering the skills in this book, you will adopt a transformative mindset that can serve you throughout your life.

Whether you are trying to figure out what you genuinely want to do professionally, what kind of culture will compliment your strengths, or even how to be a better parent and partner — this process can help. It will improve how you see yourself, clarify your expectations of others, and help you foster a sense of trust that's vital to making sound decisions at critical turning points in your life and career.

To thrive in changing times, you will have to reinvent yourself more than once in the course of your career. In fact, job change happens more frequently today than perhaps in any previous generation. And every time you change jobs, your professional agility will be tested, along with your emotional resilience and even physical stamina. The pragmatic demands of the workplace challenge all of us to succeed in ways that reflect our authentic selves.

Thankfully, the story of the *Titanic* contains vital lessons for anyone who feels stuck in a dead-end job or a professional role that stunts their potential and damages their self-esteem. This is because, when the *Titanic* sank, everything that had defined these passengers sank with it — and they were left with nothing but their innate capacity to relate to themselves and others if they wanted to survive.

They did survive, and this book shows you how to learn from their experiences and thrive.

## The *Titanic* Story: From Big Ship to Lifeboat

The *Titanic* was considered unsinkable, and so it came as something of a shock when the ship unexpectedly struck an iceberg and became fatally damaged. The crew was unprepared to abandon ship, and there weren't enough lifeboats for everyone aboard.

For those *Titanic* passengers and crew who made it into one of the lifeboats, there were new challenges. They suddenly found themselves in tiny vessels adrift in the treacherous, freezing waters of the Atlantic Ocean. In the span of a few hours, those who were still alive went from enjoying themselves aboard the largest, most extravagant luxury liner in history to facing imminent death if they didn't overcome their terror and pull together as a group.

Perhaps the most famous and well-known story concerns Lifeboat #6 and how these brave men and women managed to face their deepest fears, overcome a leadership challenge, trust one another when their lives were on the line, and take effective group action until help arrived. For today's readers, I believe many of the most relevant lessons from this part of the *Titanic* story involve how some of the individuals on this lifeboat overcame their personal fears and united as a group to beat the odds.

At first, many passengers refused to accept that the *Titanic* was sinking, and in the lifeboats, some people became overwhelmed by their emotions and unable to do anything. Some couldn't adapt to the situation and the upending of expected roles and norms. They remained stuck in what I call the "Big Ship mindset."

What makes this story so valuable for our careers today is that, on that fateful night, the survivors in that tiny vessel needed to make a fundamental mental shift if the group was going to survive. In essence, the Lifeboat Process guides us through this shift and helps us adopt what I refer to as the "Lifeboat mindset." This involves letting go of unquestioned assumptions, acknowledging danger, facing our fears, putting aside our assigned or expected roles, trusting ourselves and others, and working as a group to help save everyone.

The *Titanic* is a powerful metaphor for people today struggling to put the unexpected changes they face in their lives and careers into perspective. In this book, I have organized lessons we can all glean from these *Titanic* survivors into a process for helping clients adopt the Lifeboat mindset to explore and solve workplace dilemmas of all kinds.

For instance, in many cases, when unexpected problems threaten a company or a department, the people involved report experiencing a breakdown of norms and trust. In some organizations there is so little trust that people feel terribly isolated, disconnected from colleagues and friends, and distanced from their authentic selves. Unable to make sense of this isolation, some people make adjustments to keep themselves sane. Often, these adjustments involve striving to act like everything is just fine on the outside. However, a complex range of emotions often simmers on the inside, and if people avoid exploring and managing these emotions, the more likely they are to make a difficult situation worse by reacting ineffectively or unpredictably under stress. In a worst-case scenario, if a situation undermines someone's trust in themselves, this affects all parts of their lives, including their family and personal relationships.

Using denial to stay sane in an insane situation is understandable, if misguided. It's terrifying to discover that people entrusted to lead and safeguard our professional futures are being deceptive or are steering a company into disaster. Out of a natural desire to protect themselves, people often stop being emotionally honest, which damages their connection with their own truth. Like the captain and crew on the *Titanic* who refused to heed warnings of icebergs until it was too late, people in today's workforce can hide from and deny their own warning signs: cutting themselves off from their feelings, refusing to acknowledge problems, and avoiding taking meaningful risks on their own behalf. Often in the name of job security, people can choose to believe what leaders and others tell them is safe rather than trusting their own judgment.

The irony is that, today, *there is little to no job security.*

We all know this. How could we not? Companies go through sudden waves of downsizing or reorganization with disturbing regularity. Unexpected management shake-ups result in cultural dysfunction. Companies are acquired or merge. Funding for start-ups dries up. Scandals break out. Senior leaders are disgraced and even go to prison. Seemingly solid companies abruptly go out of business, move, or change direction.

People who cultivate the Lifeboat mindset learn to expect the unexpected, no matter how big or safe their company ship seems to be. They remain aware of potential danger and attempt to take action before it strikes. If they can avoid a problem, why wouldn't they? When they can't — and they get caught up in a tumult of change — they ready the lifeboats and prepare to survive, whatever that means specifically in their situation. Perhaps they retool their skills so they can get along in their organization as it changes. Or perhaps they jump to a new company or even a different business before it's too late.

That said, the truth is, at some point everyone will be surprised by unexpected workplace problems. We will be caught unprepared. When this happens, will we panic and deny the problem, then flounder and make things worse? Or will we recognize this situation, pause to handle our emotions and assess what's happening, then take action to foster the group effort that helps rescue everyone — before the situation becomes fatal to our job or career? Helping you manage the unexpected and survive is what this book is all about.

## The Day My Big Ship Hit an Iceberg

I, too, was once a crew member working on a "Big Ship." In the 1990s, I was the lead portfolio manager of a flagship fund for a Wall Street investment firm. I sat in a glass-walled office overlooking the trading floor, where I could observe the people on my team who were responsible for executing the positions as we bought and sold securities. I could also observe another team working for a different fund with the firm.

I remember one day in particular, which I now think of as my *Titanic* day. Things were actually going great. That morning, we chose our positions at our regular trading meeting. The trades were executed smoothly. No errors. No problems. We tracked our positions during the day. International currency markets cooperated, moving roughly in the directions we'd hoped.

High fives all around!

At the end of the day, I trudged the half mile or so back to my apartment. I walked down the hall to my apartment door, shoved the key in the lock, and turned it. At that moment, I realized something was wrong. I was feeling anxious and depressed. In spite of the smile I'd kept plastered on my face all day long as things went our way financially, I was emotionally drained.

I went inside, collapsed on the sofa, and lay there trying to understand why I felt the way I did.

Running a portfolio requires making high-stakes decisions on a daily basis. As the fund manager, the final decision was always mine. While I always did my homework, I also relied on the skills of my team. Some of the men and women in our department had more experience with the specialized securities we traded than I did, and

I had learned to rely on them for opinions and advice. Still, there were many times when the decision came down to gut feeling.

I had to learn how to listen to my gut, interpret what it was saying, and trust it enough to take action based on its signals. Often an emotion, an instinct, would alert me to something that was a little off or needed further attention; a danger had to be avoided or an opportunity leaped on.

That evening, as I lay on my couch feeling miserable, I pushed myself to examine my feelings. Why, after such a successful day, was I feeling so down and drained?

As I reviewed the day's events, the reason became clear. While my team had been whooping it up and celebrating our wins, the team on the trading desk right next to ours had run into trouble. A new hire on this team had made a significant mistake when he entered the information on a trading ticket. The error created an unintended position that went terribly wrong. It ended up being a costly financial error for our firm, and it clearly shook up this new guy and the team he supported.

As I got to the root of my feelings, I felt some relief that our team had avoided a disaster. But over the course of the evening, it dawned on me that I had still absorbed a lot of the emotional stress from this situation. Basically, I'd worn home other people's feelings like a dress that didn't fit!

The next morning I dragged myself into work, not feeling much better. I knew I was the sensitive sort, so I figured maybe my reaction was "just me." More of "my stuff." Even so, I decided to check in with my team members to see how they felt as each person dropped by my office to discuss that day's positions. To my surprise, everyone confessed to feeling exhausted and emotionally drained, too. Roger, the most macho trader on the floor, even brought up his feelings before I asked him.

"For some reason I was really depressed on the way home last night," Roger told me as he plopped into a chair in my office. "I called an old friend and we went out and got hammered. I've got a monster headache this morning."

I told him my theory that we were reacting to the pain and suffering of the other team.

"That's it!" Roger agreed in amazement. "I'd totally forgotten about that. Freaky that we'd both react to it so strongly, isn't it?"

"Not really," I said. "What's freaky is that we just assumed that a dramatic emotional situation like that *wouldn't* have an emotional impact on us."

Yet that's how many workplaces operate. People go through all kinds of emotional trials and fail to realize how profoundly they are affected by the group's energy. Instead, you're supposed to act like everything's fine, business as usual, stick to your job, and never mind that crunching sound as the Big Ship hits some unexpected object and water starts flooding in.

## Making the Lifeboat Shift

That day on the trading floor and that evening of reflection on the couch eventually led me to leave my job on Wall Street. I didn't leave in response to one incident. I left in response to a dangerous mindset that permeated our culture.

You see, on a live trading floor, you never have perfect information. You assess what you *can* know and rely on your instincts and experience to help you make strategic decisions before the market moves away from you. However, our corporate culture was inadvertently conditioning us to suppress our feelings. This was stunting an important strength necessary for making strategic decisions under pressure. This strength is vital for making the most important investment of our lives — what to do with our careers.

I departed the Big Ship of the established company — where I had been a Lipper Award–winning fund manager and had a bright future — to start my own executive coaching firm. I made what I now call a "Lifeboat shift": I realized I needed to change my mindset, and my job, in order to align my career with my values. I recognized that I wasn't living according to my authentic self, and I wanted to change my attitude and my approach to life and work.

During the transitional period that followed, I also sat down to write my first book, *The Authentic Career*. Its purpose is to help readers transcend the self-imposed limits that may have led them to narrow their professional options. As a coach and author, my goal is to help people dig deep within themselves to build careers that bring meaning to their lives.

Over the course of the ensuing decade, my clients thrived and so did my firm. In addition to coaching, I was working in executive education and doing public speaking. It was a time when many talented professionals felt they could creatively balance their personal goals and professional responsibilities in a reasonably healthy way.

Then came the 2007 downturn triggered by the subprime mortgage crisis. Most of my clients weathered the storm without losing their jobs, but there was a tremendous emotional and physical toll. I got phone calls at all hours from clients saying, "I'm okay, but the relationships between people at my firm are deteriorating due to the financial pressure we are all facing." Clients described the interpersonal dynamics with their professional peers as "crazier than a holiday dinner with dysfunctional in-laws." Clients who had reclaimed the personal power to identify what they genuinely wanted to pursue professionally felt powerless all over again.

In response, I wrote my second book, *Power Genes*, which is based on a startlingly simple premise — that power is about relationships. It's about your relationship with yourself, with other people, and with organizations. This definition of power helped my clients grasp how developing an understanding of power styles could advance their careers. It also helped them understand how their power style, and that of others, morphed under pressure — and why.

Then the winds of change shifted again.

I noticed that an increasing number of my colleagues and clients were beginning to describe different kinds of workplace challenges. These originated more from organizational dysfunctions than from interpersonal style issues. For example, colleagues I was working with at universities were reporting a values gap. Full-time faculty members described situations where there appeared to be a lack of alignment between the explicit values of their academic institutions and the behavior that was implicitly rewarded by their dean when people were being considered for tenure. My corporate clients, who had learned to navigate interpersonal relationships with agility, described a similar values gap. People in a wide variety of industries reported a crisis in corporate values. They described scenes of dysfunction and fear:

- "Our best people are getting fired…"
- "Former friends are stabbing each other in the back just to survive…"
- "It's not about what you do anymore, it's all about how you look…"
- "Forget culture and values, we have no clear direction for where our firm is heading…"
- "Peers have told me privately that they feel like they have to choose between professional survival and personal integrity to keep working here…"

Comments like these prompted me to write this book.

## How I Rediscovered the *Titanic*

In 2015, my father passed away, and my mother was living in an assisted-care facility. She needed support. To help, my husband, Charles, traveled with me to Fort Worth, Texas. The job we tackled as a team involved cleaning out the home my parents had shared for over forty years — which was also the house where I had grown up.

I felt like I faced a Mount Everest of tasks, and I had a sea of emotions to work through. Charles knew that the memories I was sifting through were heavier than any of the objects we were hauling away, so he offered to tackle the rooms on the ground floor and left me to climb the stairs to my childhood bedroom.

Still there, unchanged, were the shag carpet, beanbag chair, and LP record player of my teen years. On the bedside table — right next to where I used to lay my head — was a pile of reading material. Nestled between an old copy of *Seventeen* magazine and a science-fiction novel, I saw something that had been part of my private landscape as a girl — a crumbling old book, its spine held together by disintegrating duct tape. I found myself gently opening the volume, *The Sinking of the Titanic and Great Sea Disasters* — first published in 1912, just months after the great ship sank.

I remembered that, as a little girl, I had picked the book out of my dad's collection of naval histories. I would beg my mom or any rookie babysitter to read it to me. The book grabbed my imagination and pulled me into another world. I wondered what it would have felt like to be one of the passengers aboard the lifeboats, shivering in the dark, surrounded by people facing their demise and contemplating what their lives had meant. I imagined the small acts of courage, which aren't small at all, in life-and-death situations. I thought about how these lifeboat passengers, faced with sheer terror, must have pulled together to maintain a hopeful spirit.

There are moments when the timeline of life seems circular —

when something from your past aligns with your present in a way that seems preordained. That's what happened in that old room of mine. Suddenly, my fascination with the *Titanic* story connected with the stories my coaching clients were sharing with me. They felt alone, powerless, and adrift. They were struggling with how to work together to survive.

A couple of months prior to clearing out my childhood home, I had finished a large coaching assignment for a New York–based law firm. Due to a combination of circumstances, the law firm had abruptly announced that it would close its doors for good. There had been no warnings. No hints. Not even office scuttlebutt. The announcement came as a bombshell, and the associates and staff were stunned, unable to accept the reality, and barely able to function, let alone think about their next moves. My job was to help them deal with the shock, come to terms with the situation, and work out a strategy to move forward.

The partner who hired me told me, "Maggie, look, this is not about helping our people get their resumés together. It's not about giving them advice on networking. This is like trying to get everybody off the *Titanic* before we all go down."

An important realization took shape in my mind as I gently turned the pages of my cherished book about the *Titanic* and reflected on this client's comment. It struck me that many of the lifelong lessons that had helped me navigate my own career under pressure — and helped me guide clients through daunting times — stemmed from my early musings about those *Titanic* lifeboat survivors and how they had managed to tap into their inner strength in a crisis.

The more I reflected on the legendary sinking of the great ocean liner, the more I saw similarities between the experiences of the survivors and the experiences of hardworking professionals today.

Aboard the *Titanic*, people from all walks of life were plunged into a crisis they did not imagine in their wildest dreams. Only about a third of the passengers and crew survived. Different sources cite difference statistics, but of the 2,220 or so people who were aboard, more than 1,500 perished and about 705 managed to get aboard lifeboats. Most of those in lifeboats were saved, but the experience was terrifying and transformative. The story of Lifeboat #6 is the most famous, and over the years, it's been chronicled in books, movies, and a Broadway musical, *The Unsinkable Molly Brown*. I tell that story again in this book, but with a new purpose: to apply their lessons of survival at sea to survival in the workplace.

From my perspective, the most timeless lessons we can glean from the *Titanic* story relate to how crisis affects people — how they see themselves, how they interact with one another, and how they respond as a group when faced with abrupt and potentially catastrophic change. We all wonder, as I did as a kid: *How will I act? Will I survive? Will I behave heroically?*

## The Lifeboat Process: How to Use This Book

This book starts by retelling the story of the *Titanic*, from its launch in Southampton to the rescue of the last survivors by the *Carpathia*, and then each of the eight chapters that follow takes a closer look at certain key events and gleans important lessons for the workplace. In total, these lessons make up the Lifeboat Process. Each chapter is framed by a "lifeboat question"; these are questions we might have asked had we been on the *Titanic*, and they are definitely questions we should ask when workplace challenges arise today. These questions highlight what we need to focus on during the Lifeboat Process, and the rest of each chapter is, in essence, an answer to that question. Overall, these questions proceed in sequence and match the *Titanic* events, so that the story and the Lifeboat Process are aligned.

In addition, each chapter includes real-life examples, or "case studies," of my actual clients as they grappled with work-related disasters and used the Lifeboat Process to succeed. These stories illustrate the process in action and show how to apply the metaphor. For confidentiality purposes, the case studies use pseudonyms and are sometimes composites of several people. That said, the situations are real, as is the dialogue.

What is the Lifeboat Process? At its most basic, it's a shift in mindset, from the "Big Ship mindset" to the "Lifeboat mindset." This shift in thinking can be made anytime. It can be helpful in every aspect of our lives. But it is essential in a workplace crisis when we must act effectively with others under pressure. Metaphorically, when we hit an iceberg in our lives, we must shift our thinking from minding our own business on the "big ship" to working strategically with others to survive in a "lifeboat."

This "Lifeboat shift" in thinking changes how we relate in three ways, which will be explored in depth. First, it involves how we relate to ourselves and how we navigate our own emotions and inner challenges. When things go wrong, fear, anxiety, panic, anger, and many other difficult and unwanted emotions can emerge — which I call our "inner iceberg." Being able to act effectively in a crisis depends first on coping with this emotional and mental challenge inside ourselves; otherwise, we risk acting in self-defeating ways. If we have been conditioned by the Big Ship mindset to play our role, to do what others tell us, to not cause trouble, and to suppress our true feelings, this makes it even more important to restore our connection to our authentic selves before workplace drama undermines our professional lives.

The second area is interpersonal awareness and how we interact with others under pressure. Once the *Titanic* slipped beneath the ocean, the power structure or hierarchy of command was less important than interpersonal influence. Rank didn't matter. Personal authority won out over sanctioned authority, and informal leadership was respected over official titles. Informal leadership means trusting oneself, supporting others to overcome their fear and trust themselves, and promoting an attitude of joint effort to solve common problems, no matter what your expertise. To do this, we have to be aware of others and pay attention to all aspects of verbal and nonverbal communication.

The third area involves working with the group itself, which means leveraging the group's diverse strengths and pulling together. In a lifeboat situation, people competing with one another to call the shots can leave everyone dead in the water. Collaboration becomes a survival skill. What this means in real life depends on the circumstances, but the actions we take make a difference. The passengers on Lifeboat #6 had few resources, but they used what they had to stay warm, stay afloat, and stay determined to live long enough to be rescued. In the end, they were in the water for seven hours, which was plenty of time to despair and give up. They didn't, and the stories of how they survived through trusting one another and using their resources effectively provide timeless inspiration for us all.

Here is a brief overview of the eight questions that make up the Lifeboat Process, which proceeds step-by-step to help you operate authentically when the stakes are high:

I. **Is this ship safe?** Generations of people have been fascinated with the simple question: If the *Titanic* had been better prepared, could this tragedy have been prevented? Probably. Is your company prepared? The first step in the Lifeboat Process is assessing the environment where you work. Does it align with your values? Does it embody the

Big Ship mindset? If it's an option, should you leave now or perhaps not board at all?

2. **What do I do if I sense trouble?** The *Titanic* ignored warnings about icebergs. Even as *Titanic* launched, there were issues that led some crew members and passengers to sense trouble. But no one felt authorized to speak up or take action. However, by pausing and assessing when you notice red flags, you can recognize problems both on the horizon and in your emotional reactions to danger.

3. **When is it time to get in a lifeboat?** People sometimes deny problems or delay their reactions to them, hoping to fix them before they are noticed. Both happened on the *Titanic*, and this made the inevitable evacuation worse. Making the "Lifeboat shift" in our mindset is critical to addressing problems proactively.

4. **What if I freeze in a crisis?** The Big Ship mindset conditions us to ignore, minimize, or suppress our feelings. This can create an "inner iceberg" of difficult emotions that erupt in a crisis, causing us to freeze when we need to act. When people aren't aligned with their authentic selves and personal values, they can break down under pressure. Once a crisis arrives, the first goal is to recognize, acknowledge, and manage our own emotional response.

5. **How do I find inner strength under pressure?** When the unexpected strikes, the solution isn't in the employee handbook. Business as usual doesn't work, and the old norms don't apply. Thus, we need to cultivate the emotional agility and personal judgment to respond authentically and strategically under pressure. We empower ourselves with the personal authority to become problem solvers in a crisis.

6.  **Who can I trust in a crisis?** The first person we need to trust is ourselves, by summoning the courage necessary to admit our vulnerabilities and limits. This allows us to assess what we need to solve a problem and evaluate who within a group will help. This also cultivates the discernment necessary to clarify who to trust and why to trust them under pressure. We learn to ignore titles and status and seek to align with people who also embody the Lifeboat mindset.

7.  **How do we survive together?** The answer to this question is simple: by adopting the attitude that we must all look out for one another. We need everyone's help to pull through, and this means everyone needs to be supported and included. We treat everyone equally and don't dismiss anyone as "expendable."

8.  **What will be my story?** The *Titanic* survivors had no idea how long they'd be stuck at sea, and neither do we in our lives. We just have to keep rowing, having faith that taking the next right action in the present moment will ultimately bring success. This approach doesn't just help us survive — it ensures that we thrive. We write our stories of survival and success continually, through our ongoing actions, by adopting the Lifeboat mindset throughout our lives, rather than waiting for a crisis in order to change.

Ultimately, when it comes to our authentic leadership potential, the Lifeboat Process teaches us that, when the emotions of a group shift from fear to trust, the collective mindset shifts from self-help to us-help.

By gleaning lessons from the *Titanic* story, the Lifeboat Process helps clarify what distinguishes people who respond effectively under pressure from those who stay stuck. This isn't just related to how people think, although being thoughtful is important. This isn't just about how people feel, although cultivating the patience to identify and accept feelings is central. This is about navigating the inner challenges that arise when a crisis hits, tapping into our deeper strengths under pressure, and working with others to solve problems in ways that align with our values and authentic selves. This is foundational to charting your own course in the workplace and in your life.

The *Titanic* offers us timeless lessons about survival in any situation. My hope is that the ideas in this book will give you an even deeper appreciation for why being true to yourself is vital — because sustainable success is an inside job.

Let the voyage begin.

# THE *TITANIC* STORY:
## BIG HYPE, HIGH HUBRIS

The RMS *Titanic*, created by a collaboration between the Harland and Wolff shipbuilders and England's White Star Line, was hailed as one of the ultimate Big Ships of its day. In 1912, the cost of constructing this ship was a whopping $10 million (roughly $260 million today). One of the largest ships ever constructed, the *Titanic* was over 882 feet long, and it had a total capacity for passengers and crew of 3,547. Thanks to its advanced design and extraordinary engineering, many believed this ship to be unsinkable. The modern-day phrase "too big to fail" comes to mind.

Some of the world's most glamorous and prominent people signed up for her maiden voyage from Southampton, England, to New York. The accommodations were opulent and the restaurants were sublime. Below decks, the massive twin engines could generate enough power to drive the 45,000-ton ship at a speed up to roughly 25 knots.

The *Titanic* was heralded as being so safe and invincible that lifeboats were considered almost unnecessary. It was fitted with only twenty lifeboats. At full capacity, these lifeboats could hold only 1,178 people. Although the *Titanic* set sail with around 2,200 people on board, which was only two-thirds of the ship's full capacity, this mighty vessel still lacked the ability to evacuate everyone in a disaster.

But who knew? Who cared? Who thought that such a grand initiative could possibly fail? How could anything go wrong when people like millionaires John Jacob Astor and Benjamin Guggenheim and Margaret Brown, a prominent philanthropist, were aboard? Would they choose to travel on an unsafe ship?

Furthermore, the ship seemed to be in excellent hands. Captain E. J. Smith was a veteran mariner, commodore of the White Star Line fleet, with years of experience commanding its biggest ships. He looked the part, his chest gleaming with medals, and he played the role with reassuring confidence. This inspired everyone. The quartermaster Robert Hichens, the lookout Frederick Fleet, and the rest of the crew had complete faith in Captain Smith. All they had to do was to carry out his orders.

Besides, it was all so glamorous and fun! Great food, wonderful music. *Titanic* promised the voyage of a lifetime, and its passengers looked forward to a six-day party on the high seas. Aboard the *Titanic*, appearances were all important. As long as the skipper looked confident and the crew played their parts, passengers were encouraged to focus on state-of-the-art luxuries, which included Turkish baths, heated indoor pools, libraries, a gymnasium, and opulent cabins.

On Wednesday, April 10, 1912, *Titanic* set sail from Southampton. Crowds had gathered to watch it leave. Some hoped to catch a glimpse of the celebrities, social luminaries, and VIPs, while others gave their friends and relatives a loving send-off.

Ominously, the *Titanic* had a close call before it cleared the harbor. Due to the ship's gigantic size, it displaced 66,000 tons of water, and the *Titanic* created such a powerful suction in its wake that by merely passing downstream it tore a regular-size ocean liner, the *New York*, from its moorings. According to Logan Marshall, the seven steel cables anchoring the *New York* "snapped like twine," and this ship threatened to ram into the *Titanic*! Fortunately, the tugs *Vulcan* and *Neptune* were able to reach the *New York*, prevent it from colliding with the *Titanic*, and tow it back.

After clearing Southampton, the *Titanic* made stops in Cherbourg, France, and then headed to Queenstown, Ireland (now known as Cobh). On April 11, at 1:30 PM, the *Titanic* left Queenstown and headed for New York.

April 12 and 13 were good days on the *Titanic*. Passengers were promenading on the boat deck, lounging in steamer chairs, and patronizing the smoking rooms and card tables. By the morning of Sunday, April 14, the *Titanic* was running smoothly at full speed on what appeared to be calm seas.

Of course, as we know now, the good times were about to end abruptly.

That Sunday, as the *Titanic* neared Newfoundland, the ship's wireless room received a series of six warnings of icebergs directly in the ship's path. That night, lookout Frederick Fleet stationed himself in the crow's nest high above the deck to keep watch, doing his best with his naked eyes to scan the placid sea forward of the *Titanic*'s great bow. This was before radar and GPS, but it is noteworthy that Fleet was not even equipped with a pair of binoculars. In all the fuss over *Titanic*'s luxury, this safety precaution fell through the cracks. In addition, the ship sailed full steam ahead at a pace reported to be within a range of 21 to 25 knots. In spite of the warnings about ice in their path, the *Titanic* had a schedule to keep, and Captain Smith decided not to jeopardize it by slowing down.

The weather remained calm, with stars visible in the night sky. Some small ice configurations and mushy snow floated on the surface of the water, but Fleet observed nothing he could identify as dangerous for the *Titanic*. At 9:20 PM, Captain Smith retired to his room, but if he was hoping for a peaceful night's sleep, those hopes would soon be dashed.

Around 11:15 PM Fleet realized he saw something ominous: a huge iceberg dead ahead.

Fleet telephoned down to the wheelhouse, but First Officer William T. Murdoch, who was in command of the *Titanic* during this shift, was not there. He was out on the ship's bridge — presumably scanning the seas himself.

At this fateful moment, the wheel of the *Titanic* was in the hands of Quartermaster Robert Hichens. From his position in the wheelhouse, Hichens would have been able to hear Fleet ring the crow's nest bell, the lookouts yell out "ice ahead," and the telephone ring behind him. Yet Hichens, when he was left alone, was under strict orders not to take his hands off the wheel — no matter what! Hichens also wasn't authorized to change course until directed to do so by a superior officer. For a few crucial moments, Hichens followed protocol and did nothing, but if he had defied orders and acted, *Titanic* might have changed course in time. It was the classic nightmare of being given responsibility without authority.

As we know, when Murdoch finally yelled the order to change course, Hichens pulled the wheel over with all his might, but it was too late. The *Titanic* collided with the giant ice monolith and tragedy ensued.

In the moments after the collision, few people grasped the dire consequences of the situation. After all, who believed that anything could jeopardize the great ship? Captain Smith came to the bridge and took the precaution of calling for the emergency doors to be closed so that any flooding would be contained within segmented compartments.

At first, the passengers were not alerted to the full extent of the danger. The crew pretended everything was fine. Within twenty minutes, however, the captain was informed by his crew that the ship was critically injured. The unsinkable *Titanic* would remain afloat for only a few more hours, at most. At this point, Captain Smith activated the emergency sirens. Even then, many passengers refused to believe they were in any real peril. The sirens must be a mistake. First-class passengers who were roused from their beds and ordered on deck were still treating this situation with levity. After all, the ship was still upright.

This is the moment in the *Titanic* story where making what I call the Lifeboat shift was both literal and metaphorical. People needed to abandon ship, but this required an attitude shift. The crew and the passengers had to put aside assumptions and expectations about what was supposed to happen and deal with the reality that was quickly unfolding around them. The quicker they could get past all the attractive but ultimately false stories about the invulnerability of *Titanic*, the better. Here was the unsettling truth: The ship was going down, no one was prepared, their lifeboats were inadequate, death threatened everyone, and the only way to save as many people as possible was to work together.

This attitude shift also meant putting aside assigned roles. Passengers could not simply wait to be saved or defer to the crew's expertise; everyone had to join forces and do whatever needed to be done, whether it was their job or not. It also meant finding the inner strength to remain calm under tremendous pressure while taking effective, helpful action — knowing everyone's lives were at stake.

This human drama played out as *Titanic* was evacuated, and it continued in each lifeboat, as small groups of strangers struggled for survival in the frozen ocean, moment to moment. Some people found untapped strengths and performed heroic deeds; others succumbed to fear and self-interest and failed to help when they were needed most.

Lifeboat #7 was the first lifeboat launched off the *Titanic* under the command of First Officer William Murdoch. Although Murdoch was a seasoned leader, this lifeboat was lowered without its plug! The unfortunate passengers found themselves ankle deep in water as the cold ocean poured through the opening at the bottom of the boat.

Yet the lifeboat's passengers, including the American silent film star Dorothy Gibson, quickly fixed the problem by plugging the hole with clothing. In his famous account of the sinking of the *Titanic*, Walter Lord noted that Gibson and her mother had persuaded their bridge companions to join them on Lifeboat #7. The spirit of mutual support and goodwill among these passengers helped this group survive their harrowing ordeal together. Meanwhile, William Murdoch remained in command of Lifeboat #7 until its passengers were safely aboard the *Carpathia*, the ship that ultimately came to their rescue.

In stark contrast, Lifeboat #1 became notorious thanks to two prominent passengers who prioritized material possessions over human life. Although it had the capacity to hold forty people, Lifeboat #1 was lowered with only twelve occupants. Because they had so much additional room, several crew members on board Lifeboat #1 suggested returning to rescue additional passengers.

Yet, according to survivors from Lifeboat #1, Sir Cosmo Duff-Gordon and his wife, Lady Duff-Gordon, were particularly vocal about not wanting to return to save others; instead, these two only lamented the loss of their luxurious personal belongings as the *Titanic* sank before their eyes! When a *Titanic* crew member reminded the Duffs that at least they had the money to buy more nice things — while the rest of them had lost their livelihoods — Sir Cosmo promised to give each crew member a fiver when they were rescued.

When Sir Cosmo's financial incentive to the crew members on Lifeboat #1 was made public, the press interpreted it as a bribe. Historians are still debating whether this monetary offer from Sir Cosmo was intended as an act of generosity or to incent the crew to row toward safety instead of turning back to rescue passengers who were still struggling in the water.

## The Drama in Lifeboat #6

In the midst of all of the stories that played out on the dark waters of the Atlantic Ocean that night, one very special vessel has resonated with me since childhood. That is Lifeboat #6.

While this lifeboat had the capacity to hold sixty-five passengers, it was launched from the port side of the *Titanic* at 12:55 AM with only twenty-nine passengers on board. Most of them were women from first class.

In particular, four passengers in Lifeboat #6 have always fascinated me. Two were members of the *Titanic's* crew, and two were passengers traveling in first class. The personal struggles and triumphs these four people embodied on that fateful night have made them some of the most frequently cited *Titanic* survivors in history, and they illustrate important life lessons that form the heart of the Lifeboat Process I offer in this book.

The two crew members were Quartermaster Robert Hichens and lookout Frederick Fleet. As we know, Hichens was in the unenviable position of holding the *Titanic's* wheel at the moment of impact, and Fleet was the lookout on duty who first spotted the iceberg.

The two first-class passengers were Major Arthur Peuchen and Margaret Brown — aka, "the unsinkable Molly Brown."

Since I've already mentioned Hichens and Fleet, let's consider Peuchen and Brown.

Arthur Peuchen was a yachtsman and a personal friend of Captain Smith. As Lifeboat #6 was being lowered into the water, it became evident to Hichens, Fleet, and the bewildered female passengers huddling together in the dark that another seaman would be needed to manage this watercraft in the ocean. Peuchen volunteered to help. At the direction of Second Officer Charles Lightoller, Peuchen famously swung down the ropes as the boat was being lowered and into Lifeboat #6 to save the day!

Margaret Brown was a wealthy grandmother and divorcée who was working to help evacuate other *Titanic* passengers on the bridge. She was reluctant to board any of the lifeboats herself. Although she was traveling in first class, her passage on the *Titanic* wasn't purely for pleasure. Brown had booked this voyage to rush to the side of her seriously ill grandson.

None of these four key survivors can be classified in black-and-white terms. All of them were complex individuals with strengths and weaknesses that emerged that night. As a child, I found each of them relatable, and I pictured myself in their shoes, wondering what I would have done at each significant turning point in their saga.

I still feel this way, which is why I think Lifeboat #6 serves as such a helpful example of how crises affect us and how we can best respond. When any problem threatens our survival or our livelihoods, it upsets our expectations. In such situations we may need to evolve beyond the accepted norms of behavior to think and act differently in order to survive.

For instance, the established norms on the *Titanic* were that the crew were trained to unobtrusively follow orders, and the passengers (particularly those in first class) were entitled to a stress-free voyage where their every need would be anticipated and met. To illustrate this, consider that there were fifty butlers on hand when the first-class passengers boarded the *Titanic*. What's more, some of the more prominent travelers were also given extra staterooms to accommodate their personal servants. This voyage wasn't just marketed as an exercise in transportation; it was marketed as a dream. This marketing was so successful that, even after the crew had begun rousing passengers to get them to safety, one female passenger from first class cried out, "Lifeboats! What do they need with lifeboats? This ship could smash a hundred icebergs and not feel it. Ridiculous!"

Meanwhile, members of the crew were trained to execute their orders and remain virtually invisible to the passengers. Robert Hichens had been trained to stay at his post and do nothing until given explicit instructions from a senior officer, which can't have been easy under the circumstances. What did it take to suppress his survival instincts, hold the wheel steady, and wait for an order to change course as the *Titanic* sped toward that iceberg? Once aboard Lifeboat #6, Hichens may have been experiencing shock from this traumatic experience.

While Hichens had served as a quartermaster on many vessels and had extensive experience on the high seas, he fell apart emotionally once aboard Lifeboat #6. As the crew member designated to lead these lifeboat passengers to safety, the people on board initially turned to him for guidance, help, and reassurance.

They didn't get it.

Shortly after reaching what seemed like a reasonably safe distance from the big ship, Hichens became unable to communicate with his fellow lifeboat passengers effectively; he wasn't willing to lead by example and wouldn't even help them row! Instead, Hichens froze at the helm of the lifeboat, wrapped himself in a blanket, and started babbling out loud about how dismal their chances of survival were.

Clearly, this wasn't helpful, and his fellow passengers quickly lost confidence in Hichens, most likely because Hichens had lost confidence in himself.

When it came to collaborating with his fellow seamen, Hichens also appeared to be threatened by Major Peuchen's military bearing, social standing, and knowledge of boats. What began as bickering between these two men about what to do and when to do it quickly erupted into a power struggle. Eventually, the norms separating passengers from crew broke down completely on Lifeboat #6.

Then, something unusual happened. The leadership vacuum on Lifeboat #6 got filled in an extraordinary way.

Margaret Brown, a grandmother with no naval training, began to take matters into her own hands. Defying any formal chain of command, Brown helped her fellow passengers pull together, stay warm, and get organized to survive the night. When Hichens tried to assert his authority, the group shut him down. Gradually, everyone else in Lifeboat #6 started following Brown's informal leadership, including Peuchen and Frederick Fleet. Both supported her guidance of the group with their seamanship.

History has judged Hichens harshly, as did his fellow lifeboat passengers, who later assigned him unflattering monikers like "the coward" and "the pessimist." This judgment of Hichens stands in sharp contrast to the compassion and gratitude that the survivors from Lifeboat #6 exhibited toward their other fellow passengers.

Today, I'm more interested in understanding the pressures brought to bear on Hichens, and how they impacted his behavior, than on vilifying him. As a child, when I read Logan Marshall's account, I would say to myself, "I'd never react like Hichens!" But as an adult, I know better. I know what it's like to be in a no-win situation, to give my power away, to freeze when I should act, and to be less than my best self under pressure.

I'm also interested in Margaret Brown's emergence as the informal leader on Lifeboat #6. Why her?

After all, Arthur Peuchen was eager to take control! He was a successful businessman and had served as the vice-commodore of the Royal Canadian Yacht Club. Why wasn't *he* the leader the other passengers turned to for inspiration when the old norms gave way and a life-and-death struggle to survive ensued?

Ultimately, these individuals and the dynamics of the group overall provide dramatic lessons in personal transformation and effective action under pressure. The story of the *Titanic* has always been associated with adventure, endurance, and even romance. It also embodies how we can survive and thrive in our lives and careers today.

## Lifeboat Question #1

# IS THIS SHIP SAFE?

The first question we ask before boarding any ship is "Is it safe?" We also ask this same question, in a variety of ways, before joining a company: *Is this a good job that I can depend on? Can I succeed at this job, and will it help grow my career? Is this a stable, well-run company? Will it stay in business? Are there dangers or warning signs?*

Of course, we can't predict what will happen in any job, company, or sea voyage, but we try to make the smartest, safest choice possible based on what we *can* know. When it comes to navigating career and workplace challenges, the start of the Lifeboat Process is awareness: What kind of company are you employed by, and what is your situation? Are you in an organization that's operating with a Big Ship mindset?

Let's clarify something important at the start. What defines a "Big Ship" isn't necessarily size. It's the culture, the organizational mindset. While some large companies certainly fall prey to the Big Ship mindset, as we shall see, some don't. It's important to bear in mind that any size firm can be susceptible. This mindset was perfectly embodied by the *Titanic* as it set sail.

## *Titanic*: The "Unsinkable" Ship

Who doesn't want to be transported by a larger-than-life fantasy? Who doesn't secretly long to be part of something greater than ourselves? Whether the solicitation is being made to sea travelers or job seekers, the basic urge to be part of something exciting often tempts people to get on board a "big ship."

Many of the early advertisements heralding the maiden voyage of the *Titanic* were presented to the public via vibrantly illustrated travel posters designed to compel people walking by to stop, look, and get excited. These posters, many of which are impressive examples of the way a powerful image can create brand advertising, are quite valuable today due to the fact that the White Star Line pulled down and destroyed as many of them as possible after the *Titanic* sank.

Following this tragedy, the source of the widespread belief that the *Titanic* was "unsinkable" was debated both in a formal inquiry and in the press. It was discovered that this claim was never explicitly made. The earliest roots of it have been traced back to a special edition of a London trade publication called *The Shipbuilder*. In 1911, this quarterly journal released a special edition featuring interior photos of the *Titanic's* private promenade and first-class accommodations. This article proved to be strategic because, even though the bulk of prospective *Titanic* passengers were of humble means seeking a better life, this glimpse of opulence filled a vital psychological craving. The *Titanic* wasn't just a vessel that would transport you to another continent, this voyage could transport you to another state of being!

The actual claim made in the 1911 article was: "As far as it was possible to do so, these two wonderful vessels [*Titanic* and its sister ship, *Olympic*] are designed to be unsinkable." In practical terms, this claim was based on the construction of the *Titanic's* hull, which was subdivided into a series of sixteen supposedly watertight compartments. The theory was that, even if the hull was punctured, any water that flooded into the ship could be sealed off in the specific compartments that had been breached. Theoretically, this meant that the ship could stay afloat long enough for all of the people on board to be rescued. Sadly, because the designers at Harland and Wolff didn't want to interfere with the spacious passenger areas higher in the ship, the walls of these watertight compartments were not made high enough. As a result, the ship ended up flooding and sinking before help could arrive.

Looking back, it's clear that if the focus on safety hadn't been dwarfed by the wave of enthusiasm for the sheer luxury that *Titanic* represented, any claims about the ship's invulnerability would have been recognized as overblown. No ship is greater than the ocean and its power.

But it wasn't just publicity and public enthusiasm. The people central to *Titanic's* conception, construction, and operation also made choices that contributed to the tragedy, and these decisions reflected the "Big Ship mindset" this chapter examines. Learning to spot this mindset is vital to making sure whatever ship you board and the company you work for is safe.

In fact, the *Titanic* was plagued with troubles before it ever left port. During the week prior to its maiden voyage, the *Titanic* was berthed in Southampton, and all the final arrangements were being rushed. There was a scramble to finalize all of the details in first class to meet everyone's high expectations. Then, thanks to a coal strike in Britain, crew members were instructed to take coal out of other liners to gather the six thousand tons of coal *Titanic* required for this voyage — the show must go on! To cap this off, the ship was being inspected by the Board of Trade. Without getting a certificate of clearance from the Board of Trade surveyor, the whole spectacle would come to a grinding halt. While the world watched and the international elite packed their finest, the *Titanic* was almost not granted clearance to sail.

Here's why: Crew members had discovered a coal fire in the bottom of bunker #6 on the *Titanic* that had been there since the ship had completed its brief sea trials in Belfast. They couldn't put this fire out. This presented a significant risk because bunker #6 was close to the *Titanic*'s hull, and a fire here could potentially weaken the hull's structure. If something struck this particular spot while the ship was at sea, the integrity of the vessel would be compromised.

According to the documentary *Titanic Arrogance*, if the surveyor from the Board of Trade had known about the fire in bunker #6, the *Titanic* never would have been granted clearance to set sail in the first place. Of course, the ship *somehow* did manage to pass its inspection, but we don't know why.

There's a good chance, however, that the bunker fire was kept hidden, and that this decision was made by the people at the top: Thomas Andrews, a Harland and Wolff designer; Captain E. J. Smith; and Bruce Ismay, head of the White Star Line. They knew about the coal fire and that acknowledging it would cause a world of problems. How long would it delay the launch? Would they have to refund everyone's money?

Ultimately, they chose to take a calculated risk that turned out badly. The maiden voyage took place on schedule while the coal fire continued burning. The precise details of how the *Titanic* passed its inspection remain one of history's unsolved mysteries.

Further, after the remains of the *Titanic* were discovered on the ocean floor, historians noted that the place where the iceberg sideswiped the ship is eerily close to a black spot on the hull near bunker #6 where that uncontrollable fire was blazing. What are the odds?

But finger-pointing isn't the goal. Rather, the decision to set sail despite problems — while violating official regulations and putting others in harm's way — reflects the same type of flawed thought process that still operates in the business world today. Anyone who invested with Bernie Madoff, worked at Enron, or went down with the ship at Arthur Andersen can attest to that! By learning to spot this type of flawed decision-making, we can be better prepared when *we* are faced with tough professional choices. This type of awareness not only saves our careers, it can make our departments and firms safer places to work.

Let's take a closer look at these three men to clarify what may have been driving their thought process under pressure.

First, Thomas Andrews was the head of the drafting department for the Harland and Wolff shipbuilding company. Andrews was in charge of the team that chose to make the doors on those watertight compartments too short. Andrews was aboard *Titanic*, and after the iceberg was hit, Andrews was the guy who did the calculations to figure out how quickly the *Titanic* would sink and who informed Captain Smith.

As for Captain Smith, he had a colorful track record of accidents and near misses at sea. His peers described him as "a bit of a chancer." That said, he was extremely popular with the millionaire elite — and the White Star Line considered catering to this crowd vital to the venture's success. To his credit, Captain Smith acted heroically in the final hours of his life; he saved as many people as possible and then went down with the ship. But he also made several "calculated gambles" — like ignoring the bunker fire — that led directly to the tragedy.

Finally, the head of the White Star Line, Bruce Ismay, was considered a captain of industry. He had negotiated the joint venture with Harland and Wolff that had led to the creation of the *Titanic* and its sister ship, *Olympic*. Ismay was also aboard during *Titanic*'s maiden voyage, and he apparently tried to convince Captain Smith and the ship's chief engineer, Joseph Bell, to do a speed test. Ismay's input was one of the key reasons the ship maintained full speed in spite of the ice warnings that were being received the night the ship sank. Ultimately, unlike Andrews and Smith, Ismay managed to save himself and survive the tragedy. In the final moments, he boarded collapsible Lifeboat C and was later picked up by the *Carpathia* along with the rest of the survivors. Afterward, Ismay was vilified in the press for saving himself instead of following the "women and children first" principle. In spite of being officially cleared of blame after the disaster, Ismay spent the rest of his life plagued by a deep depression from which he never fully recovered.

The actions of all three men embody what the Big Ship mindset represents. They appeared to be so caught up in the story that had been created about their ship that they became unable to fully acknowledge and assess risks and to respond appropriately to changing circumstances. This mindset can influence both individual behavior and an organization's overall culture.

*Titanic* historians tend to agree that Andrews, Smith, and Ismay all displayed behavior prior to the *Titanic*'s maiden voyage that indicated a sense of personal invulnerability. Perhaps this is because they had internalized the narrative that *Titanic* was unsinkable, and so they began to feel indestructible themselves. This would help explain why all three men traveled on the ship in spite of the risks they knew of and were hiding from others. They didn't think their lives were in peril, since they fully believed that the ship they had created could get through anything. This would also explain why they evaded official safety regulations. From their perspective, these regulations were pesky details that could easily be dismissed in the service of a voyage that was going to make history. Similarly, the warnings about icebergs weren't taken seriously enough to incent them to slow down. They rationalized jeopardizing everyone's lives, including their own, because all three believed the story about *Titanic*, which they had helped script. They weren't just hiding the risks involved — they were denying them.

The Big Ship mindset often promotes a grandiose attitude, in which the ends justify the means, and people can lose touch with the value, and vulnerability, of human life.

In the corporate world, once this attitude takes root in a firm's culture, people stop paying attention to details, listening to feedback, and looking for risks. If people don't believe there are any dangers that can harm them, they stop looking for dangers. When people become attached to beliefs in their own greatness, they ignore, minimize, and reject any criticisms, since they feel they are beyond criticism. When this type of thinking goes unquestioned for a prolonged period, it can lead to catastrophic failures that result in many people going down with the ship. Learning how this mindset takes root can prepare you to make wise career decisions — particularly under pressure.

When it comes to your career, you want to get on the right boat in the first place. When it comes to assessing whether or not your ship is safe, you want to ensure that the people in charge strategize with a sense of humility, listen to feedback with an open mind, and remain flexible and teachable in the face of new information.

By definition, people who think they already know everything are unteachable. This attitude is dangerous both on the high seas and in the business world because it hampers the awareness and agility necessary to course-correct when unexpected events unfold.

For some, belief in personal invincibility can become like a drug. It helps people rationalize operating in a self-serving manner because they convince themselves that what they are trying to achieve is so compelling. Just like addiction, the more people operate in a self-serving manner, the more they engage in denial. They reflexively resist self-reflection and the evidence of danger.

Belief and denial are powerful forces.

One reason denial is powerful is because it frees us from the need to take responsibility for our behavior. However, it often arises when we become attached to a false narrative or a false inner self. We buy into a fiction that we are better than others, and so we defend that sense of self, even when doing so denies reality.

We know how this played out with the *Titanic*. The leaders and people in charge who should have known better, who should have questioned the very concept of "invincibility" and proceeded with caution, did just the opposite. Flawed decision-making defined their approach and their response to changing conditions, and they did not realize these flaws until it was too late. Only once the worst happened did they recognize all the ways they'd blinded themselves to potential disaster.

## The Big Ship Mindset

It's important to learn to recognize the Big Ship mindset in a firm's culture. You may recognize signs of Big Ship thinking in your company's CEO, in your boss, in your coworkers, or even in yourself. The key warning sign to be alert for is when this type of attitude becomes normalized by a critical mass of people running the show.

Often, the Big Ship mindset begins with the seductive twin promises of safety and importance: Not only won't this company fail, but it will dominate and perhaps even revolutionize the industry. In themselves, those promises aren't bad, but question them, and watch out for the warning signs of passivity, blind acceptance, defensiveness, and denial.

Typically, people operating under the sway of the Big Ship mindset follow three simple rules that block their awareness of what's happening in their inner world. Becoming conscious of these rules and learning to question them when warranted is foundational to making the Lifeboat shift.

### Big Ship Rule #1: Remember Your Role and Always Play Your Part

This Big Ship rule says that you've got a part to play — but only that part — in a story that's been scripted for you by others. This conditions people to dutifully play only the role they have been assigned, even when circumstances change. This leads people to ignore reality and embrace denial. On the *Titanic*, many passengers initially refused to get on a lifeboat because they assumed that the situation couldn't possibly be that bad. These passengers had internalized the belief that the *Titanic* was completely safe because they had been told that it was, and as passengers, their role was to passively enjoy the ride. Even in a life-and-death situation, many of them were unwilling to question this belief and to take charge of their fate until it was too late. In corporate America, this same devotion can cause people to stay in dead-end jobs for far too long.

### Big Ship Rule #2: Always Stay Busy

This Big Ship rule invites you to normalize what's happening when your mind starts racing under pressure. This unhelpful reflex in your inner world is connected to the unspoken assumption that, if you aren't rushing around constantly, something is wrong. Underlying this is the feeling that you have to constantly prove your value. After all, if your value is based on how you appear to others, why would you ever stop performing?

What's more, nonstop activity produces adrenaline, and adrenaline is a drug. Not only does a steady stream of adrenaline coursing through your system buffer your feelings, it also makes it possible to ignore your body's need for rest and relaxation. Ignoring your physical needs helps you perform the duties others expect of you with more mechanical consistency.

A temporary perk of adrenaline is that it offers an emotional energy boost. Unfortunately, it's an illusory feeling that must be constantly pursued.

### Big Ship Rule #3: Faster Is Better

Another rule of the Big Ship mindset is that "faster is better." While the *Titanic* wasn't trying to beat a record on its maiden voyage, speed still mattered to their image. They wanted to stick to a tight schedule. Because of this focus on speed, the captain and crew on the *Titanic* missed some important signals. Those of us today who feel compelled to respond impulsively to the latest voicemail, email, or even tweet can relate.

Moving too fast can lead to snap judgments — both of ourselves and others. Snap judgments can be costly because they are often rooted in fear.

Some of the professional challenges we face are due to external pressures imposed on us by others. Other challenges are due to the internal pressures we put on ourselves, and many are a combination of both.

It's easy to see how any one of these Big Ship rules could hamper our authentic success. However, the real mischief starts when we put them together. Combining these mandates leaves us cut off from what's going on in our inner world, so that we ignore the warning signs of trouble until it's too late.

## LIFEBOAT CASE STUDY
### *Corey Looks Before He Leaps*

Here's an example of a client of mine whose understanding of the Big Ship mindset kept him from getting on an unsafe boat!

Corey, a trader who was working through the Lifeboat Process, used his growing understanding of the Big Ship mindset to help him ask better interview questions. Corey had sought me out after making the decision to leave an investment firm that he felt was taking excessive risks with investor funds without fully disclosing the implications of some of their more controversial trading positions.

A family man committed to modeling sound values for his children, Corey was focusing the sharp intellect he had previously used to beat the market on what he considered one of his most important decisions — finding a healthy place to invest his time and energy for the next segment of his career.

Recapping one of his interviews, Corey told me, "Based on your suggestion, I asked a fairly prominent hedge fund CEO how he handled challenges from people who disagreed with him."

"How did he answer?" I asked him. I often suggest that clients use this question to help evaluate a suitable workplace.

"He told me that he never has challenges," Corey replied with a smile. "He went on to add that people who cross him have challenges, but that he's always fine. The gleam in this guy's eyes as he said this to me was scary."

"Was this a red flag for you?" I asked Corey.

"Not only did I decide to pass on the job, I made a polite excuse to leave our lunch early, grabbed the next flight available, and came home," Corey told me. "If I could have found a place to get a drive-through exorcism before hugging my kids, I would have considered it."

The hedge fund CEO who interviewed Corey was expressing values distorted by Big Ship thinking: He refused to acknowledge the value of feedback that might alert him to potential problems, and he seemed ready to deny problems if they arose. In classic fashion, he wanted to project an image of invulnerability, but this attitude, and his readiness to dismiss those who might raise warnings, meant he was likely to hit an iceberg — which is exactly what happened.

Shortly after Corey passed on this job, the hedge fund CEO popped up in the news when he was cited for regulatory violations. Even though this hedge fund had flunked a key audit, the CEO had basically ignored the problem, continued to market aggressively without addressing the underlying issues, and was allegedly looking for a scapegoat to finger for the unflattering press his firm was garnering.

Bullet dodged, Corey!

## The Personal Impact of the Big Ship Mindset

Even as the business environment churns and companies go through all kinds of disruption, many of us still cling to the idea that being aboard a Big Ship ensures safety and stability. Just as the *Titanic* passengers did, we buy the messages and the hype and make the assumption that, if we work hard and stick to the program, the organizations we support will provide many of the things we need to survive and thrive, from healthcare benefits to a sense of professional identity. The Big Ship promises to give us a reason to get up in the morning, the money we need to pay our bills, and clarity about where we stand in the pecking order of life.

To succeed and prosper, we know we have to comply with the unwritten rules. Play our part. Look busy. Everything will be *fine* — even more than fine — so long as we keep our noses to the grindstone and don't make waves.

When our existence is defined by the Big Ship — whatever its description — our sense of inner self starts to become defined by the outer role we play. This is true whether our particular ship is a too-big-to-fail firm, a well-funded start-up, or a small private business. All types of companies can reflect the Big Ship mindset, which asks us to trust that leaders know what they're doing and ignore any evidence otherwise.

Even if the company avoids hitting icebergs and sinking, the Big Ship mentality entails a tremendous hidden cost to employees. We sacrifice our authentic self to fit in, survive, and succeed. Our genuine values can evaporate. Our sense of our own worth may center on how others react to us and on feedback from people who don't really know us.

The result: We feel cranky, competitive, and unfulfilled, and we internalize the Big Ship mindset. We don't acknowledge our feelings. We ignore problems. Many clients tell me that they feel they can't speak truthfully about anything, even to themselves, for fear of what the consequences might be.

This is true for staff members, managers, and senior leaders. Top executives ignore problems because they can't handle feelings of vulnerability or admit mistakes. When key staff members sense this about their leaders, they may start planning their exit strategies because they sense that something is wrong and there could be trouble ahead.

That is how I felt in my Wall Street job.

It's important to pay close attention to these warning signs. To do so, you need to increase your awareness of the situation and learn to recognize when the firm's culture has normalized the Big Ship mindset. Ask yourself, "What kind of ship am I on?" Describe the ship for yourself, as *you* understand and see it, not how others — your colleagues, managers, marketers, analysts, the media — describe it.

There are all kinds of ships. As one of my clients put it, "I feel like I'm on a pirate ship. The leaders loot the spoils and live in luxury. The rest of us share offices so small we can barely concentrate on a client phone call. If you ask for the resources you need to work effectively, or complain in any way, you're likely to find yourself walking the plank!"

In fact, the Big Ship mindset doesn't want you to recognize or acknowledge any problems. Everyone in a company wants to believe that the ship they are on is safe. This shared passion to believe all is well can start to eclipse people's individual ability to sense when things aren't quite right. Other ships may fail, but people start to convince themselves that *their* Big Ship won't make those mistakes — perhaps because, like the *Titanic*, it's too big, dominant, and advanced to fail. The Big Ship mindset encourages us to push aside our emotions and *ignore our feelings.*

What feelings?

The feelings that get stirred up when we realize that not everything we're hearing makes sense, whether in our company, our work environment, or even in our own head. The feelings that make us long to do something that's personally significant and to cultivate our authentic talents. The feelings that draw us toward others who are actively engaged in work that fulfills a sense of purpose. The longing for a sense of meaning in life that's bigger than the next paycheck.

Oh…those feelings.

We take back our personal power when we start tuning in to our feelings, speaking our truth, thinking for ourselves, and interacting

with others in a way that fortifies our personal integrity and en-
hances our capacity to trust.

Organizations whose internal culture falls short of their fancy
slogans and splashy websites are hiding behind a false self. Like any
false self, this will foster a fear-based emotional climate.

The group energy of a workplace has a pervasive impact on everyone, and this extends into every facet of life. The values normalized in the workplace will color our attitudes, and the way people
react to us on the job will influence our sense of self. Our workplace
can even recalibrate the speed with which we move from moment
to moment throughout our day.

## LIFEBOAT CASE STUDY, PART 1
### Mark's Denial

Mark had been working in the pharmaceutical industry for almost
two decades. He had worked for several companies as a sales executive and believed that he would always have a place in the industry.

After several years working at one of the major pharma companies as a senior manager, Mark had been enticed to join a start-up in
an executive position with equity ownership. Mark didn't feel that
taking this job was a risky move. The company was well-funded
and had a promising new drug in the pipeline. Mark felt his professional values were completely aligned with those of the firm's CEO,
Robert. Having known Robert for several years, Mark felt this start-up
was in good hands. The board members were stars, big names in industry and finance. His compensation package, which included generous benefits and stock options, would potentially ensure that he
was financially secure for life — if he just kept things on track. That
appealed to Mark, who was married with two tween kids.

Mark felt safe.

Soon after he joined the company, however, things began to change.

First, the chair of the board, Stephen, a well-known partner in a venture capital firm, made it known that he was not satisfied with the company's progress. Stephen's dissatisfaction stemmed from his desire to get his money out faster than planned. From Mark's perspective, Stephen also seemed to want an unrealistically high return on his investment.

Within days of Stephen announcing his timeline for cashing in at the firm's board meeting, Robert departed the company with no warning. Was the CEO fired? Did Robert resign? No one knew.

Stephen, a man with no background in pharma, stepped in as acting CEO.

Mark understandably felt uneasy. Things weren't right, but he didn't want to talk about the situation with his wife or his friends. He was not alone. Colleagues were reluctant to talk about these changes as well. Soon, Mark found it hard to sleep at night. He felt tension in his back. When he spoke, his voice grew tight.

Still, Mark told himself, everything would be okay. After all, stuff happens all the time, right? He wasn't about to quit. The company had plenty of financial reserves. The board of directors was solid. The product was almost ready to launch.

Then Stephen informed the leadership team that they had new sales targets and objectives that were much more aggressive than their previous goals. At the same time, Stephen cut costs to the bone, including much of the budget Mark needed to get the word out about the product.

Mark felt responsible for the financial well-being of the salespeople he had brought on board. He frequently cast himself in the role of protector when it came to those he supervised, and one of the rules he lived by was speaking truth to power when warranted.

Mark decided to spend a week on the road visiting the doctors who were projected to be the top clients for this drug; he wanted to get their feedback to the management team before the firm got too far off course strategically.

Sounds logical, right?

Proceeding with the objective professionalism that is his hallmark, Mark sent Stephen a respectful and succinct email outlining the feedback he would be soliciting and requesting some time to brainstorm before he left. He also asked Stephen for the opportunity to present his findings at their upcoming management meeting.

The first sign that trouble lay ahead came when Stephen — whose daily communication pattern tended to involve multiple email requests punctuated by testy calls if things weren't moving fast enough — went silent.

Mark gave it a couple of days, figuring Stephen was probably swamped. After all, this guy was the CEO. If he was retreating behind closed doors and clearing his calendar, there was probably a reasonable explanation.

An arrow in Mark's traditional quiver of professional tools was the simple fact people tended to like him. An easygoing man from a loving family, Mark came across to others as genuine because he *was* genuine.

Mark made the next logical move. He walked down to see Stephen's administrative assistant, Angela, to find out when he could schedule a meeting.

Angela made her "I'm sorry" face the minute she saw Mark heading her way. "He's in a bad mood today," Angela mouthed cautiously.

"Did he read the email about my trip?" Mark asked.

"He did, and I don't think he's going to meet with you," she cautioned. "However, he scheduled a slot in the management committee meeting to address your feedback."

"Good enough for me," Mark responded affably. "Let him know I dropped by and that I'm heading out tomorrow. I'm sure he's swamped."

Angela nodded sympathetically and said, "Safe travels."

Mark made the trip and, when he returned, wrote up a report and prepared a presentation for the senior management team.

What could possibly go wrong?

The tongue-lashing Mark received from Stephen at the management meeting showed him. Mark was used to debating statistics, questioning data, and listening to the priorities of others. But he wasn't used to being in the crosshairs of a CEO who sarcastically trashed his skills and his reputation in front of his peers.

In the meeting, Mark tried to make what he believed were relevant points, and each time, Stephen cut him off by erupting in a character-assassinating temper tantrum. It was stunning, and Mark wasn't the only professional caught off guard. A couple of the division heads tried to defend Mark so they could hear what he had to say, but Stephen shot them down as well.

Before the meeting, Mark had copied a resignation letter on his thumb drive, and he had joked with some trusted friends that, if Stephen didn't listen to reason, he was ready to walk out on a moment's notice.

The problem was, Mark realized he wasn't ready to quit. He felt responsible for his team and their futures. He also had his family to consider.

Things went from bad to worse over the next few weeks. Stephen would not listen to dissent, questioning, or bad news. He demanded that people massage their numbers and reports to make it look as if everything was going fine. If anybody challenged him, he would call them out. He was an expert at placing blame.

Stephen started making fun of Mark and questioning his abilities in front of others on a regular basis. Eventually, Mark began to question himself. What if Stephen was right? What if he wasn't as accomplished and respected by others as he liked to believe he was? What if he was a wimp for not being able to meet Stephen's targets? Was it really so bad to massage the sales numbers? If he quit, would he be able to get another job?

Mark no longer felt safe in the company, but he was so cut off from his own feelings, his colleagues, and the company's mission that he could barely assess the situation. He felt alone, afraid, and much too scared to make a move.

As I discuss in chapter 2, Mark had hit an "inner iceberg" that was damaging his self-confidence and self-esteem and keeping him from acting on the danger he sensed. This danger threatened everyone in the company. Mark knew that Stephen wanted him to play the role of a "yes man." He also began to believe that Stephen would fire him, and perhaps even try to destroy his reputation, if he didn't fall in line. Mark and many of his colleagues felt like they were watching their organization go under, one wildly bad management decision at a time, and yet their warnings were being ignored, refuted, and denied.

In this situation, Mark froze. As I have seen with many clients in similar circumstances, Mark became passive and just hoped that *somebody* would take control and that *somehow* things would get back to normal.

That, of course, is not how to avoid a catastrophe. Especially when it comes to our own careers, we can't wait until someone in authority tells us to turn the wheel.

Mark realized he needed help, and he reached out to me for coaching after listening to one of my podcasts.

"When I heard you say, 'You can have a good career if you're smart, but you'll only have a great career if you're brave,' I decided to call you," he told me.

"Why did that statement prompt you to reach out?" I asked him.

"Because I can't figure out what's brave and what's reckless right now, and this isn't just about me. The choices I make are going to affect others, and reality has changed for all of us."

Mark had reached the point where he was willing to face his feelings head-on and take action.

He was ready to make the Lifeboat shift.

## Lifeboat Question #2

# WHAT DO I DO
# IF I SENSE TROUBLE?

One reason the story of the *Titanic* disaster has such enduring appeal is that it is an object lesson in the need to question perceived reality, trust our gut, and when necessary, act on our own personal authority to save others and ourselves. This is what I call the Lifeboat shift: the moment when we see or sense danger and realize that the ship we're in is headed for trouble. This is the moment when we realize that "business as usual" will no longer work, and we must take emergency action, whether to avoid the danger or to abandon ship.

Making this shift requires several things, the first of which is trusting our own eyes, ears, and intuition. Life's most important decisions often require more than logic. Where to work, how to invest our retirement savings, who to marry: We can't know the outcome of our decisions when we make them, and we can't know all the risks and obstacles we'll face. Indeed, many problems are like icebergs. At first, issues may seem small and insignificant — we see only the tiny tip — and we must guess how big and dangerous they really are or might become and how urgently we need to move to avoid them. When deciding what to do, we must tap into our intuition and sometimes even take a leap of faith.

This is hard in a crisis. Many clients have told me that, as pressure mounts within their organizations, they find themselves emotionally numb. The more cut off they become from their feelings, the less energy they can summon to take meaningful risks on their own behalf. They freeze, they act out, and in worst-case scenarios, they end up making compromises that erode their ability to operate in alignment with their genuine values.

Thus, when you spot an iceberg and recognize trouble ahead, the first and most important thing to do is to pause, tune in to your feelings, assess your reaction and the problem, and then focus on doing the next right thing in the present moment.

## Danger on the Horizon

In the early 1900s, competition among the various shipping lines was fierce, yet the commitment to the value of human life remained uppermost among vessels at sea. Hence, it's not surprising that the various ships that entered the treacherous waters of the Atlantic radioed one another frequently with ice warnings.

The *Titanic* received no fewer than six iceberg warnings from other ships sailing in their vicinity on April 14. The first one came in at 9 AM from the *Caronia*. During the formal inquiry following this tragedy, it was reported that this warning from the *Caronia* was the only one that was posted where all of *Titanic*'s officers could see it for formal consideration. When Captain Smith saw this first warning, he asked Sixth Officer James Moody to calculate when the *Titanic* would reach the ice indicated in this report. Moody reported that this would be around 11 o'clock that evening.

So what happened to all the other iceberg warnings?

This simple but crucial question takes us to the wireless room of the *Titanic*, where the senior wireless operator, Jack Phillips, was engaged in a task that was starting to overwhelm him. As soon as the *Titanic* got within radio range of Cape Race, Newfoundland, Phillips was finally able to establish direct communication with the continent of North America. While passing on iceberg warnings was a critical part of his job, Phillips had also been tasked with promptly relaying messages from *Titanic's* passengers to friends, relatives, and business contacts. This was critical to keeping the passengers happy, and the backlog was such that he wasn't able to pause, prioritize, and focus on the relative importance of the various types of messages that were flowing in and out.

In other words, Phillips was losing perspective on what was truly important — safety.

At 9:30 PM, the nonstop personal messages were interrupted by an ice warning from the *Mesaba*. This warning didn't strike Phillips as urgent since he had already passed on earlier warnings, and these hadn't prompted any feedback from the officers in command. Phillips, who was swamped, figured things were under control.

In retrospect, they weren't.

About fifteen minutes before the *Titanic* struck the iceberg, an urgent message from the *Californian* burst into his headphones. "Say, old man," boomed wireless operator Cyril Evans from the *Californian*, "We are stopped and surrounded by ice." The *Californian* was about twenty miles away from the *Titanic* at the time.

Phillips was running on fumes at this point and responded impatiently, "Shut up! Shut up! I am working Cape Race." Phillips felt he *had* to keep up with those passenger messages to keep everyone happy.

It's a tragic irony that disaster might have been avoided if the wireless operator hadn't been too overworked to think more clearly under pressure and prioritize safety. To his credit, the frustrated and exhausted Phillips quickly got back to the *Californian* with the message, "Sorry. Please repeat. Jammed to Cape Race."

Tragically, by this point, the *Californian's* receiver wasn't able to get a message clearly from the *Titanic* anymore. Soon after, at 11:35 PM, Evans shut down his wireless and retired for the night.

Of course, wireless warnings from other ships weren't the only means used to assess potential threats.

That night, Frederick Fleet and his partner, Reginald Lee, were the two lookouts in the *Titanic's* crow's nest. These men probably both felt like they'd drawn the short straw when it came to their tour of duty on that freezing night. While the passengers below were enjoying the comfort of their warm beds, Fleet and Lee were out in the elements striving to keep their freezing eyelashes from hampering their ability to scan the waters ahead.

Fleet wasn't a Big Ship thinker. He couldn't afford to be. Fleet was responsible for trusting his vision and seeing danger in time to alert others. An experienced seaman, Fleet knew that spotting an iceberg could be tricky business. While icebergs could sometimes be identified by a ring of white foam that formed around the base when waves broke against it, the seas were calm that night. Sometimes the reflection of the moonlight made it possible to see the white surface of an iceberg in the distance, but there was no moon that night. At least the stars were bright — that seemed helpful. What wasn't helpful was the fact that, as noted earlier, the *Titanic* had left Southampton with no binoculars for the lookouts.

Neither of these two men in the crow's nest were happy about that oversight.

Around 11:30 PM, Fleet casually mentioned to Lee that the horizon ahead had seemed to develop a slight haze. It seemed so subtle at first that he almost didn't mention it. A few minutes later, Fleet made a horrifying realization. Sometimes icebergs appeared as black objects, and one was directly in their path!

Fleet rang the bell in the crow's nest three times to alert the crew on duty and telephoned the wheelhouse immediately. Despite their best efforts to warn the crew in time, Fleet and Lee were subjected to the horrifying experience of watching the iceberg coming closer and closer while the *Titanic* maintained its course at full speed.

While historians still debate the precise details of why it took the crew so long to respond to Fleet's warning, Fleet is regarded as having done everything he could under the circumstances. His warnings arrived in time to still avoid the crash, so what happened? Where were the officers in charge?

Only three people were authorized to change the course of the ship: Captain Smith, First Officer Murdoch, and Second Officer Lightoller. When Fleet telephoned the wheelhouse, the only officer present was Quartermaster Robert Hichens, who was duty bound not to release the ship's wheel or turn the ship. By then, Captain Smith had retired for the night, Lightoller had been relieved of command by Murdoch at 10 PM, and Murdoch was out on the bridge.

Theoretically, this still shouldn't have presented a problem. That's because two additional officers were always supposed to be stationed in the wheelhouse with the quartermaster to make sure everyone communicated in a crisis and orders were relayed promptly. The two additional officers assigned to the wheelhouse on that fateful shift were Sixth Officer Moody and Fourth Officer Joseph Boxhall.

Where were they? As luck would have it, just before Fleet spotted the iceberg, Moody had left to run a quick errand. At the same time, Boxhall had decided to run out for a quick cup of tea. After all, it was freezing! What could possibly go wrong!?

The human dimension of this would be touchingly funny if the consequences weren't so tragic.

The minute they realized the ship was in harm's way, Moody and Boxhall both rushed back to the wheelhouse. Moody grabbed the wheelhouse phone, Murdoch yelled the order to change course, and Hichens turned the wheel with all his might.

At first, it seemed like the *Titanic* might just clear the danger. Then, as the iceberg moved alongside the starboard bow, survivors report they heard a strange scraping noise.

This was the sound of impending disaster.

Remember this whenever you hear the refrain "it can never happen to me." Even seemingly small errors can result in catastrophic failures.

Nearly all my clients confirm that signs of trouble arise at companies long before they hit a metaphorical iceberg and these firms go under. The end may come suddenly, but for months, if not years, many employees have seen the writing on the wall. This is especially true when company leadership subscribes to the Big Ship mindset. That is, senior management refuses to listen to or address the concerns of employees, who are expected to do their jobs and nothing else. What's worse, some Big Ship thinkers punish people who "rock the boat" and raise bad news by demoting or even eliminating them. Thus, to keep their jobs, employees play along and maintain the illusion that everything is okay when they know it's not.

To foster compliance and distract employees from problems, senior management sometimes uses chaos as a control tactic. Having employees dash around collecting endless and confusing data, hiring and firing consultants, and nonstop travel often ensure that everyone remains exhausted and unavailable for frank discussions.

In this type of scenario, people operate on autopilot. They aren't authentically present. They lose touch with their feelings, and this can infect someone's entire life and leave them unprepared to handle a crisis. Like Robert Hichens, if that person suddenly must make critical decisions under pressure, they may freeze or break down — sometimes experiencing outbursts of temper or becoming tongue-tied and unable to make any decisions.

This is a critical lesson from the *Titanic*: In any kind of crisis, it's important to be as fully and authentically present as possible. When you sense trouble, don't panic and freeze. Train yourself to pause and assess.

## Pausing: The Gateway to Emotional Wisdom

Pausing is a foundational skill for navigating life. Pausing enables us to spot incoming threats and dangers as well as to remain calm in a crisis so that we avoid panic and act effectively. Any time strong emotions are triggered, we should pause to assess our feelings and what's causing them. Sometimes we only need to pause long enough to take a deep breath and stem the rush of adrenaline coursing through our system, which may be prompting an excitable rather than an effective response. Other times we might choose to pause for days or even weeks to regain perspective and decide on the most strategic way to proceed. I recommend practicing the art of pausing until it becomes emotional muscle memory. This particular skill is essential for reclaiming our personal power in any situation, and it's particularly helpful under stress.

Pausing is a skill that can be learned.

Over the past twenty years, I've worked with people who have grappled with a wide range of emotional triggers on the job that prompted unhelpful reactions. Some clients are self-described people pleasers who find themselves giving their power away by anxiously filling in conversational silences. Self-described alphas also give their power away, but their reactions are often different. When problems arise (sometimes due to damage they've done), alphas often find themselves reacting impulsively, talking *over* others, trying to force solutions, or setting unrealistic targets for their teams. Whatever your behavioral pattern happens to be, mastering the ability to pause will help you stop reacting emotionally and start responding strategically.

Anyone can learn to pause. That means *you* can learn to pause. That said, mastering the skill of pausing can involve a tricky learning curve.

Why?

Because this is an experiential skill. You can't learn to pause under pressure by imagining yourself doing it. You have to actually *do* it, over and over, and this takes courage.

For people who have been conditioned to operate from the Big Ship mindset, pausing can feel like turning up a dimmer switch in a dark room. When people have made a habit of avoiding their emotions — perhaps by engaging in nonstop activity or endless chatter — pausing forces them to experience their feelings. This can be uncomfortable, and they often report battling thoughts like, "Isn't this self-indulgent? Aren't we wasting precious time? I'll just *say* I paused, but I'm not going to waste time *doing* it!"

Pausing can be scary because people don't always know what they are going to find when they pause long enough to look within. With practice, people start to understand how pausing can help them clarify any self-defeating thoughts or self-sabotaging behaviors that may have been undermining their performance on the job.

When our bodies are flooded with adrenaline, our immediate impulse is to act first and think later. Pausing is about doing the opposite.

It's worth it.

When you pause, that adrenaline gets redirected so you can focus more clearly on what's unfolding in the present. For example, people who manage to steer clear of a potential car accident and pro athletes who are able to excel under pressure focus intently on what's unfolding in the moment. This focus is so intense that people sometimes say it feels like time is *slowing down.*

This is the ultimate mastery of pausing, which allows people to be aware of their inner selves and manage their emotions while simultaneously responding strategically to whatever is going on.

Mastering the ability to pause is a skill that benefits everyone, not just top athletes. And similar to how athletes work hard to maintain their physical agility, you practice pausing to cultivate your *emotional agility.* That way, as pausing becomes a habit, you know you will be able to handle yourself in a crisis. This builds self-confidence and trust in yourself, which will then be reflected in your interactions with others.

Pausing is the opposite of operating on automatic pilot. People operating on automatic pilot do what they are told without question so long as an authority figure reassures them that everything is "fine." Instead, by pausing, you evaluate circumstances for yourself. You listen to your internal guidance. This increased awareness improves your ability to act effectively in the moment.

Pausing helps you take your power back from the inside out.

## Spotting Your Inner Iceberg

Operating with wisdom means being aware of what's unfolding in our outer world *and* our inner world. That's because, if we've been conditioned to suppress our feelings or distract ourselves from things we'd prefer not to notice, we can't make authentic decisions.

In our professional lives, it isn't just outer threats that can derail our career. Internal threats can sink our ship as well.

In the Lifeboat Process, I refer to the inner emotional mass of self-doubt, distraction, fear, and anxiety that strikes in response to an external crisis as an "inner iceberg." Just like the tip of an iceberg, what we notice about the emotions that build up inside us under stress is often only a fraction of what's beneath the surface. Inner icebergs grow the longer people refuse to acknowledge how they truly feel — even to themselves.

Some of us grapple with inner icebergs that leave us frozen in fear at the very moment we should be summoning the courage to act — whether that means speaking up, planning for the future, or taking necessary risks to save ourselves.

Here are some examples of people grappling with an inner iceberg:

- The shy internal auditor who feels anxious about speaking up when he or she discovers that a senior executive at the firm may be handling expenses inappropriately.
- The human resources executive who hides the fact that key talent is leaving the organization over what they consider unfair compensation.
- The marketing executive who is so confrontational in staff meetings that he or she doesn't get frank feedback or innovate ideas necessary for the firm to remain competitive.
- The computer programmer who would rather isolate and write code than do the networking necessary to advance to a management position.

As these examples show, inner icebergs can prompt emotional reactions that keep us stuck and prevent us from growing. They can build up over time when we suppress feelings we don't want to face. When we pause, we start to recognize them and ultimately shrink them.

When you hit an inner iceberg, you may find that these suppressed feelings come flooding in hard and fast. You don't realize how much they've built up, and you're unprepared for how strong they are. As a result, rather than responding strategically to avoid a collision, you crash.

Unfortunately, these can become career-sabotaging moments. When people have felt alone and invalidated for too long, sometimes they simply don't care anymore. When this attitude takes hold, they may lose perspective and release their pent-up frustrations in a way they later regret.

Of course, the key to professional success is learning to identify inner icebergs *before* we hit them! This is why the Lifeboat Process starts with pausing under pressure. We train ourselves to pause when difficult feelings arise and identify them, rather than suppress them. We accept those feelings and explore them; we ask questions. If you struggle to speak up, are you looking for external validation before offering opinions? If so, why? When someone annoys you, assess whether that reaction is objective and fair. If not, why not? Do others at work share your reaction to that person? If so, will that group conflict become an "iceberg" that damages the functioning of your team and the future of your organization? If so, what can you do to avoid that danger?

## How Are You Communicating with Yourself?

Most senior executives I've coached quickly grasp that effective communication is vital to success. As they prepare for presentations and team meetings, business leaders know that staff members will be both listening carefully to the specific information they convey, such as proposed budgets, and focusing on the speaker's body language, vocal tone, and even pace.

Body language telegraphs to others what we're feeling, and it involves things as simple as breathing, posture, and gestures. No one I've worked with has ever disputed the assertion that nonverbal expressions of confidence often convey more than the actual words used.

But eyes widen when I point out that body language and breathing are ways your body communicates with you. This is particularly important when you are off stage and the only audience is yourself.

In other words, in order to identify inner icebergs, as well as to understand their source, it's important to become more conscious of the nonverbal ways you embody and communicate emotions. These are critical signals people often miss!

Right now, your body is communicating your inner experience. Notice where you are, how you are sitting, and how easy it is to stay focused in this moment as you read.

Many people get so caught up in their heads that they lose the connection to the wisdom of their bodies. When you pause, don't just analyze a situation or your feelings intellectually. Let yourself feel your emotions, and notice how they feel and express themselves in your body. What is your body communicating about what is going on? Sometimes, we are so distracted by the thoughts racing through our minds that we aren't actually feeling.

Learning to trust your gut under pressure involves becoming genuinely curious about what you are feeling and why. The more you are conscious of what's happening in your inner world, and the signals your body may be sending you, the less likely you are to give your power away under pressure.

## LIFEBOAT CASE STUDY, PART 2
### Mark Takes Back His Power

At the end of the last chapter, we noted that Mark's reaction to the behavior of his new CEO, Stephen, had flooded him with a paralyzing sense of self-doubt. Mark's Lifeboat Process began with examining how he felt and what he did on the job when he felt pressured to play the "yes man" to stay safe. Whenever he felt triggered, he learned to pause and assess: What was he feeling? How was he reacting? When was he abandoning his own truth? Why was he often tempted to give his power away, and what *was* that power, anyway?

As Mark began to experience the difference between operating according to the Big Ship mindset and embracing the Lifeboat approach, he was struck by how easily he had minimized his own feelings in the past.

Like many well-trained professionals, Mark was practiced in the art of communicating with others. But under pressure, he ignored the messages he was sending himself.

Stephen's dramatic tirades, combined with Mark's conditioned response to defer to his CEO, often left Mark feeling mute, fearful, and exploited. The more his CEO's verbal assaults battered his psyche, the more powerless Mark felt.

Mark's Lifeboat work involved objectively assessing what happened to the way he communicated with himself during Stephen's outbursts — and how these reactions impacted what he did in the moment, since these responses were often neither effective nor strategic. Instead of beating himself up for not having the perfect response on cue, Mark learned to tune in to his feelings and spot physical tension in his body.

The more Mark worked on quietly observing his own reactions, rather than getting caught up in the adrenaline rush of Stephen's latest rant, the calmer he became during management meetings. Mark was starting to reconnect with a felt sense of his innate value on the job.

Stephen sensed this, and he didn't like it. This was a CEO who used chaos as a control tactic, and he liked it when his team hung on every word he said with a sense of urgency.

"You're really bugging me today," Stephen snapped one afternoon as he glared at Mark across the conference table.

"What's wrong?" Mark asked calmly.

"It's like everything I'm saying is just washing over you — like you don't even care!"

"That's not the case," Mark replied evenly. "It's just that I'm listening to the way you are interpreting the data we've collected on projected sales, and I simply don't agree with you. I definitely care."

The silence that followed felt like checkmate. Mark's tone was respectful, even, and subdued. The other division heads, who were also grappling with how to deal with Stephen, suddenly looked at Mark with hope in their eyes.

Mark felt an inner rush of self-esteem, and Stephen ended the meeting promptly.

The power of the Lifeboat Process is that it isn't just about outer work; it's about inner work. The Big Ship mindset often dismisses emotions: If other people can't see it — it doesn't count. However, when we are operating from the Lifeboat mindset, inner work is essential and usually comes first. Only after we recognize our "inner icebergs" and release frozen feelings can we see and understand external problems clearly enough to choose the most effective, strategic course of action.

Stephen was a bully, and like many bullies, he had developed keen instincts for how to "divide and conquer." Prepared to lash out verbally at any moment, Stephen relished the ability to keep others so anxiously focused on him that they were too distracted to think of anything other than what they needed to do to placate him.

Over time, Stephen's management style had left Mark and many other staff members so drained that they unconsciously let Stephen define their value. If he said they had done a good job, they were on top of the world! If he berated them, they often beat themselves up for the rest of the day.

As Mark silently observed the waves of self-doubt that washed over him when Stephen put him in the crosshairs, he shifted from self-doubt to self-discovery. Accepting these feelings without judging himself opened the door for him to consider Stephen more clearly. Gradually, Mark stopped taking Stephen's comments personally and saw them for what they were, emotional manipulation. As Mark reclaimed the power to define his value from the inside out, he could evaluate Stephen's criticisms more objectively. Sometimes, Stephen's assessments were completely wrong, and sometimes they had merit, but the way he treated others undermined Stephen's effectiveness as well as employee morale. In fact, Mark increasingly used Stephen's actions as leadership lessons on what *not* to do under pressure.

"I'm actually beginning to enjoy this!" Mark reported after a couple of weeks of tuning in to his feelings. "While Stephen has still been erupting all over the place, I've been monitoring my relationship with myself rather than buying into his hyperbole. Instead of feeling like I want to crawl into a hole and disappear, I've noticed that sometimes I'm tensing up to keep myself from laughing. When he gets really wound up, it's begun to feel like watching a spoiled kid jumping up and down and calling me names on the playground."

"Are you sleeping better?" I asked him.

"Much," he replied with relief. "That said, I'm still pretty sad about something."

"What's that?"

"Now that I'm not as preoccupied with every little mood swing Stephen is having, I'm noticing the impact he is still having on the rest of the staff," Mark replied. "It's like watching military recruits line up trembling for a testy little dictator. It's tough to stomach."

"Give it time," I told him. "Your courage is growing, and emotions are contagious."

## Acceptance and Trust

Another lesson from the *Titanic* story, which Mark learned first-hand, is that you can't help other people until you learn to accept and trust yourself. By acknowledging our feelings and treating ourselves with dignity, we learn to conduct ourselves in a calm and focused manner that demonstrates genuine self-esteem under pressure. Setting this type of tone on the job inspires the trust of others. The more fear dissipates and trust takes root in the relationship we have with ourselves, the more our presence contributes to an emotional climate that makes this possible for others. Like any emotion, trust is contagious.

I've always wondered what it must have felt like for the *Titanic* passengers huddling together on Lifeboat #6. I imagine everyone must have experienced a felt sense of one another that was so primal that it can't be fully captured in words. The challenges of that fateful night plunged these individuals into such an intense experience of the present moment that none of them had the luxury of distancing themselves from their feelings. Through intuition, instinct, or even subtle physical clues, they knew who was tired, who was scared, and who they could trust to row for another hour.

In practice, trust is more than a mental concept. Actual physiological changes take place when people feel more trusting. Their facial muscles relax, their shoulders get less tense, and sometimes they even audibly exhale as they feel less defensive. Trust isn't a logical decision; it's an emotional response that registers in our bodies as well as our minds.

Many hardworking people have told me that they believe being emotional means being out of control. In my view, this belief is limiting. We all experience emotions. That's part of being human. We don't react ineffectively because we have feelings. We give our power away because we don't know how to deal with our feelings effectively.

While feelings can be a source of vulnerability, they can also be a storehouse of inner wisdom and a source of inspiration. Cultivating an authentically powerful relationship with yourself comes from genuine acceptance of what you are feeling in the present moment without judgment.

My job is never to get clients to listen to me — it's to train them to listen more clearly to themselves. There's a nonverbal dimension to listening, and that's where the subtle cues from your body guide you to the emotional wisdom needed to reclaim your personal power.

## Improving Your Relationship with Yourself

Ultimately, we shouldn't wait until we are triggered to practice pausing and to learn to assess what's going on in our inner world. Listening to, accepting, and respecting ourselves is a lifestyle strategy that will improve our lives in innumerable ways. For instance, consider what we do when we want to create a great relationship with someone important. Whether it's a personal or professional relationship, here are some common things we do to put our best foot forward:

1. We listen to the other person carefully so we can learn as much as possible about them.
2. We validate this person so they feel emotionally supported and good about themselves in our presence.
3. We are thoughtful about all aspects of how we communicate with them, from our body language to our tone of voice to our word choice.
4. We are mindful of selecting the best time and place to

be with this person so they will enjoy themselves in our presence.

Of course, we do many other things to build strong relationships, but reflect on these four and how you may have used some of them in the past to cultivate a relationship with someone important to your career. For example, one client explained that he would routinely devote the time and energy necessary to travel for meetings with sales prospects at favorite restaurants near their homes. This wasn't just to simplify the commute for his prospects; it was because he hoped these potential clients would experience a sense of ease by meeting in a place where they often spent time with friends and family.

With this in mind, consider what you currently do to strengthen your relationship with yourself.

How carefully do you listen to yourself? How do you talk to yourself under pressure? Do you validate yourself when you make a mistake, or does a harsh voice start barking orders in your head? How much "quality time" do you spend with yourself, and how do you spend it? What do you do to honor yourself for a job well done?

One of my clients, Alex, found himself struggling with the demands placed on him when he was granted sole custody of his seven-year-old daughter, Sarah. As the store manager for a large sports marketing firm, he found that managing an employee training program and managing his daughter's school schedule left him with virtually no time for himself.

A hard worker, Alex was surprised and pleased when he got an unexpected bonus for an after-school program he had initiated where parents and their kids got together to test some of the sports equipment he was selling. Baseball mitts, tennis rackets, and even fishing rods were flying off the shelves thanks to his email campaign to get parents off the bench and outdoors right along with their kids.

As he looked at his bonus check, Alex had a great idea about what he could do to spend more time with Sarah on the weekend — and to simultaneously enhance his relationship with himself. Alex asked Sarah if she'd be interested in helping him build a small pond in their back yard. Sarah, a shy young girl who was still recovering emotionally from her parents' divorce, eagerly agreed. While Sarah wasn't particularly drawn to sports, she loved crafts and building things!

As they worked together — visiting the quarry together to buy the stones, then digging the hole and figuring out how to keep it full and clean — Alex told Sarah stories of how he used to walk on the beach and watch the seagulls to clear his head when he was her age.

Now, every morning before he drops Sarah off for school, Alex makes sure he gets up twenty minutes early to have coffee on the bench by the side of the pond they built together. Alex told me that he has his best ideas there because, when he's by the water, he's able to listen to himself much more clearly.

People who have been operating from the Big Ship mindset deal with life from the outside in. They tend to turn to other people for approval, security, and even love. Rather than taking full responsibility for partnering with themselves, they often live as if the quality of what's unfolding in their inner worlds requires little or no attention or upkeep.

An unfortunate side effect of this personal neglect is that they tend to make important life decisions to please others rather than making choices that truly reflect who they are on the inside. All sorts of mischief can result from this — not the least of which is that people who habitually operate this way tend to sell themselves short! Improving your relationship with yourself makes it that much easier and more natural to pause under pressure, assess what's going on inside, and make effective, authentic decisions about what to do next.

Toni, a warehouse supervisor for a large East Coast distribution center, discovered that learning to pause and listen to herself more thoughtfully was vital to performing effectively in her role.

While she was widely respected for her industry knowledge and her straightforward approach to team management, Toni found herself tongue-tied and squirming like an anxious teenager whenever she was invited to present to senior management. Talking to the top brass was a trigger for Toni that led her to collide into an inner iceberg of fear and doubt. The night before she was scheduled to make some brief remarks to the firm's president, Toni literally broke out in hives!

By learning to pause under pressure, Toni quickly realized that she was putting so much pressure on herself to showcase her hard work that she couldn't relax and communicate effectively in these situations. Through learning to become aware of what the signals from her body were telling her, Toni was able to make an important discovery about her relationship with herself.

As she focused on staying present and breathing calmly when she was triggered, Toni noticed that memories of having to work twice as hard as her little brother to get any validation from her parents flashed through her mind. Toni's parents had immigrated to the United States from Eastern Europe, and she had been raised in a family where women were conditioned to defer to male authority.

In fact, Toni's father once told her that they couldn't afford to send her to college. Since her little brother was the man of the family, they would need to save for his education. Toni would have to fend for herself.

She did.

Toni got a part-time job, put herself through community college, and entered the workforce. From her first day at her first job, Toni worked tirelessly, attended every training program she was eligible for, and established a reputation for being a dedicated worker.

Interpersonally, however, she found herself struggling with authority figures as her career progressed.

As Toni progressed through the Lifeboat Process, she realized she had suppressed her anxious need for recognition by working harder than anyone around her for most of her life. Unfortunately, her emotional craving to be noticed was creating so much inner tension that she wasn't able to express herself effectively when it mattered most to her career.

By learning to listen more thoughtfully to herself, Toni gradually found that she was able to stay more present for what was unfolding around her during senior management updates. As she practiced pausing, she also practiced strategic listening. Through learning to trust herself under pressure, Toni trained herself to tailor her comments to members of the senior management team so that she could convey the information they needed with precision.

By learning to pause and listen more thoughtfully to herself, Toni's need for external validation lessened. Her inner iceberg began shrinking. This was a huge relief in her personal life as well. For much of her life, Toni had dreaded family dinners. This was because her mother fawned all over her little brother (who was now living in her parents' basement) and consistently minimized Toni's accomplishments. To her surprise, this wasn't bothering her anymore.

When Toni's firm went through a reorganization, the new

senior management team decided to review the files of their thirty warehouse supervisors and select three to join a select focus group to help them run the firm more effectively. Toni was delighted when she learned that she had been selected.

Thanks to the shift she had made in her relationship with herself, Toni became valued firm-wide as someone who got to the point without grandstanding. As her story illustrates, listening to ourselves with patience and compassion is foundational to achieving sustainable success.

*Lifeboat Question #3*

# WHEN IS IT TIME
# TO GET IN A LIFEBOAT?

I f the company we work for, like the *Titanic*, ever hits a fatal iceberg, we don't want to be among the clueless passengers and crew blithely "rearranging the deck chairs" when we should be abandoning ship. However, at first, few people aboard the *Titanic* realized how serious their situation was. Many passengers barely registered the crash and kept enjoying themselves as if nothing had happened. While the first lifeboats were being lowered, crew members minimized the danger even as they prepared passengers to evacuate. Most people assumed they'd be saved.

Thankfully, not every organization will necessarily go under just because they hit a few obstacles or encounter problems. Not every iceberg is fatal. However, in our professional lives, the question remains: At what point should we decide that the damage to our company or our job is so serious, the danger signs so alarming, that we should prepare for the worst?

Because there was no chance of repairing the ship, the *Titanic* isn't a perfect metaphor for every type of professional challenge.

Rather than "abandon ship," we can use the Lifeboat Process to re-define our role at our current firm, rebuild professional alliances, and help the organization's culture evolve. That said, others may find that leaving the ship they are on for another vessel is the best course of action. Whatever unfolds for you, it's important to bear in mind that making the Lifeboat shift isn't about whether or not you stay at your current firm. It's about what you do when you realize circumstances have evolved to the point that you need to reassess your situation, along with your mindset, your behavior, and your approach.

The most important thing to evaluate when assessing whether or not to remain with your firm is the leadership team's capacity to change when the company struggles, for any reason. The *Titanic* might well have avoided disaster if the captain and crew had been willing to heed warnings sooner, take more thorough safety precautions, and change course before it was too late. Similarly, observe your company's leaders and the overall company culture: How do people respond to danger signs and to the inevitable accidents and disruptions that hit any business, whether the troubles are in the marketplace or in the workplace? Do responses embody the Big Ship mindset or the Lifeboat mentality?

Part of making a wise choice about whether to stay on board or leave comes down to evaluating the capacity of a company to adapt to changing circumstances. Once you lose confidence in that, it may be time to plan an exit strategy. Of course, no one can predict when a problem will prove fatal, but often, the Big Ship mindset itself is what ultimately dooms an enterprise.

### Captain Smith Makes the Lifeboat Shift

As a kid, one of my favorite parts of the *Titanic* story was the drama that unfolded during the ship's evacuation. The part I found partic-ularly inspiring involved the actions of Captain Smith and Major

Archibald Butt, a military aide to the president of the United States. Major Butt was traveling as a first-class passenger on the *Titanic*, and he and Captain Smith became personal friends over the initial days of the journey.

Roughly forty-five minutes after the *Titanic* struck the iceberg, Tom Andrews managed to calculate how long the *Titanic* was likely to stay afloat. As a result, Captain Smith and the senior officers had a clearer sense of the magnitude of the tragedy enveloping them. There were punctures on the starboard bow, water was flooding in, and the compartments were filling fast.

Hoping he had at least an hour and a half to get as many passengers onto lifeboats as possible, Captain Smith's priority was to ensure that no one panicked. We don't know exactly what information Smith and the crew shared with the passengers or whether they believed that the nearest vessel, the *Carpathia*, might arrive before *Titanic* sank. Nobody knew who would live and who would die at that point. What we do know is that, as water kept coming in, passengers started going out.

The stewards on each deck were instructed to knock on cabin doors to tell passengers to dress warmly, get their life jackets on, and proceed to the deck. Rather than sparking terror or panic, this unexpected news was greeted with annoyance by some passengers. Remember, they had been told this ship was unsinkable — and they believed it.

Before the officers were dispatched to their lifeboat stations, Captain Smith called them into his office and gave each of them a gun. These firearms were to be used by the officers to protect themselves and other passengers if, and only if, there was a rush for the lifeboats. Clearly, Smith had embraced the gravity of what they were all facing. He also realized that, if panic ensued, countless more lives could be lost.

Having been instructed to help passengers board the lifeboats, Quartermaster Robert Hichens rushed to the first-class promenade deck to start readying one of the collapsible boats. When he was ordered into one of the regular lifeboats on the forward side, he jumped into Lifeboat #6 to help get it filled with passengers and ready to leave.

As everyone assembled on the deck and the sense of urgency grew, the scene became increasingly chaotic. The crew struggled to get the lifeboats lowered properly, and they struggled to get passengers into them. By this point, Frederick Fleet had also been ordered into Lifeboat #6 to help row, and he was encouraging female passengers to climb over the rail and get on board.

It wasn't an easy sell.

The huge ship, which still had functioning lights, looked much safer to many of these women than a small lifeboat wobbling down ropes into the vast, dark ocean below. What's more, the emotional tension of tearing themselves out of the comforting arms of their loved ones proved daunting.

There are multiple heartbreaking accounts of women not wanting to leave their husbands and being encouraged by the men they loved to save themselves. As they were lowered onto the lifeboats, many women were terrified, hysterical, and in tears. Some women were injured climbing aboard; others were practically thrown to safety.

Where were Captain Smith and Major Butt in all of this? They were next to each other in the middle of the chaos working as a team to maintain a sense of calm and save the lives of others. By joining forces to save as many lives as possible, one passenger at a time, Smith and Butt made the Lifeboat shift in real time. They weren't denying the problem or plotting to save themselves at the expense of others; they were united by a shared commitment to save "women and children first" and keep panic at bay.

In Logan Marshall's account, he describes eyewitnesses who saw Captain Smith take his friend Butt aside and whisper something in his ear. We will never know what was said, but it's likely that Captain Smith made it clear that he wasn't going to be taking a seat on any of the lifeboats. After this conversation, Major Butt became not just inspired — he appeared transformed, as if he had been given a command. Eyewitnesses described an immediate change in Butt's expression and bearing. After that whispered conversation and up to the moment the ship plunged under the water, Butt took charge of getting others to safety. He helped startled sailors untangle ropes, he calmed frightened women with an aristocratic, courageous tone, and he helped Captain Smith maintain order as they worked together to ensure the safety of as many people as possible.

To me, this part of the *Titanic* story is vital. While the Big Ship mindset may have prevented Captain Smith from objectively assessing the risks that arose and then acting with appropriate caution during their journey, Smith displayed in his final hours his capacity to evolve — to act bravely, compassionately, and selflessly — and ensured that his final voyage was a credit to his legacy.

The lesson is this: Even when a particular leader or a specific organization is operating by the Big Ship mindset, don't write them off as incapable of making the Lifeboat shift. We don't really know what people will do in a crisis, and everyone's behavior may change under pressure, for better or for worse.

While the circumstances and stakes are admittedly very different, I have had the rare privilege, as an executive coach, of witnessing senior management and company leaders display the same strength of character in a crisis as Captain Smith. When their companies have floundered, I have seen Big Ship executives make dramatic Lifeboat shifts. Many of them have shown unexpected displays of compassion, gratitude, and generosity toward their surprised employees, whose livelihoods were threatened by changing circumstances. Witnessing these moments has taught me that you never have the full measure of another person until you see how they handle themselves in a crisis.

Of course, it would be better if leaders made this Lifeboat shift sooner, right? Before they hit an iceberg? Indeed, we might ask, how high do the stakes have to be to snap someone out of their Big Ship mindset for the good of their firm? It depends. Everyone is different. Some people embrace the Lifeboat mentality easily, some need the heat turned up pretty high emotionally before they "tune in" to their inner worlds, and some never make this shift.

Making the Lifeboat shift isn't always easy. It requires self-awareness, a certain amount of soul searching, and a willingness to make sacrifices for others. These sacrifices often involve more than money. As I explore in a later chapter, there are moments when making the Lifeboat shift requires us to put aside roles and status and align ourselves with values that serve the greater good.

Further, the nature of the choices any of us need to make in order to embody a Lifeboat shift varies depending on our jobs, our responsibilities, our lives, and the circumstances. Yet in both ourselves and others, it's important to recognize small acts of kindness, moments of sincere self-reflection, and initiatives that build teams rather than resumés. We don't have to wait for a crisis to recognize patterns of behavior that signal someone who could make a Lifeboat shift in an emergency, nor do we have to wait for a crisis to start embodying a Lifeboat mentality.

Let's face it, one reason the story of the *Titanic* has enduring appeal is that it shows how people sometimes become their best selves when the stakes are highest. Heroes never go out of style. Naval and political leaders like Captain Smith and Major Butt, along with civilians like Margaret Brown, saved and inspired others through their nobility and courage under pressure. There were many heroic men and women from all walks of life who, in their final hours, exemplified the Lifeboat mindset in action.

However, in your professional life, a good way to decide whether to stay with a company or to leave it, hopefully *before disaster strikes*, is to pay attention to how the leaders in your company behave under pressure and to the organizational culture they create.

## The Big Ship Story: Business as Usual

Every company tells an inspiring story about itself that embodies how it came to be and the company's purpose or goals. Often, there's a "brand story" conveyed by the firm's website, marketing brochures, and ad campaigns. These public stories can tell us a lot about a company, but not everything.

An organization's internal communication patterns also convey a story. This private story reveals important clues about how the company really operates. As the *Titanic* story shows us, the private story sometimes differs in important ways from the public one, and recognizing the internal story can help you evaluate how well any senior management team, and the company itself, can adapt to unexpected challenges.

Often, when things aren't going well, internal communication patterns can be your best clue as to whether the firm is mired in Big Ship thinking or evolving toward the Lifeboat mindset.

When Big Ship thinking prevails, and problems arise, the impulse is often to deny or minimize any problems and pretend that it's business as usual. The journey must never stop! Full speed ahead! The message must always be consistent. To attract talent, positive press coverage, and eager investors, the image of success must be maintained, even if that image doesn't reflect the full truth.

Thus, in order to deny or hide real problems, Big Ship leaders manipulate the story. They focus on distractions to keep from looking within, both within the company and within themselves. As Big Ship leaders become invested in these increasingly false narratives, they can lose their connection to what's real and to their authentic selves. They begin to believe they are the roles they are playing, and their sense of self becomes fully invested in the image they project. When keeping up appearances becomes more valued and more rewarded within the company than telling the truth — it may be time to jump.

## Big Ship Problem Solving: Ignore, Deny, Blame

What does the Big Ship approach to dealing with problems look like in practice? At its most extreme, when problems arise in a company wholly devoted to the Big Ship mindset, dealing with them tends to go through three stages:

**Stage 1: Ignore What's Happening:** Just like when *Titanic* was first warned about nearby icebergs, leaders at various levels may know there's a problem ahead, but they try to minimize it. They convince themselves and others that the problem isn't serious, that it won't come to pass, or that the company can handle it without needing to slow down or change course. What's more, they often instruct others not to talk about it. No one needs to know! Don't worry the staff or panic customers!

In some cases, employees have already internalized this instruction: They know to play their role and to automatically censor any information that may make the people in charge uncomfortable. No memos come out and no preventative measures get taken. What's senior management doing? They are crossing their fingers and hoping that as long as no one acknowledges the threat, it will go away.

Stage 1 can take a long time to unfold.

**Stage 2: Deny What's Happening:** As we all know, when problems are ignored, they often tend to get worse. If everyone has ignored a problem for a while and it just keeps popping up, people operating from the Big Ship mindset may start denying that the issue was ever a problem in the first place. If someone within the organization tries to confront this denial, he or she risks being dismissed, rebuked, or belittled. At this point, denial can devolve into bullying. Some Big Ship bullies may hope to brainwash their staff into accepting their denials as reality, while others may just want the subject dropped. When Big Ship bullies identify a person they can't intimidate or silence, that person may be seeing a pink slip soon.

Meanwhile, as the dark cloud of denial settles over the corporate culture, everyone involved gets caught up in playing their assigned part and keeping their heads down. Emotional honesty goes underground, trust dries up, and the stress of suppressing the truth puts everyone on edge and triggers outbursts.

Eventually, denial of a genuinely serious problem can't be maintained; the damage is too great. That's when the final stage begins.

**Stage 3: Find Somebody to Blame:** When a problem can't be ignored or denied any longer, and a genuine crisis arrives, Big Ship executives often prefer to assign blame than to take responsibility for fixing the problem and figuring out how to help those who are hurt by the disaster. Sometimes, to save themselves, they simply leave. Big Ship executives often have a luxury speedboat waiting so they can escape if their company can't be saved. In many cases, people committed to denial race away to take over another Big Ship.

However, bear in mind that people can respond in unexpected ways in a crisis. Both Captain Smith and Bruce Ismay displayed a similar Big Ship mindset up until the moment *Titanic* hit the iceberg, and then their behavior changed dramatically. Captain Smith made the Lifeboat shift and focused on helping women and children onto lifeboats, while Ismay was busy getting himself off the *Titanic*.

That said, long before a company reaches a crisis point, there are many clues we can glean about how safe the ship is by paying attention to how people handle all kinds of problems — big ones and little ones. Does this firm have an "all hands on deck" culture, or is everyone on the bridge pointing fingers at one another while the water pours in? As a rule, do people tend to place blame or accept responsibility? Are tempers short or is cordiality maintained under pressure? Are expectations reasonable? Do you find you have to devote a good deal of time and energy to shielding yourself from negative energy as you wade into your office to get your job done, or are you inspired by the tone set by your colleagues as you face challenges together?

Here's an important warning sign to bear in mind: If people around you are so anxious about keeping their jobs that they sacrifice the ability to speak their truth, know their own minds, and operate with trust and integrity, it's time to lower your lifeboat into the water and get the oars ready.

## How Big Ship Thinking Shapes Our Values

As I've said, the Big Ship rules stress playing your part, staying busy, and moving fast! The authority of the people in charge is unquestioned, and if anyone expresses feelings, thoughts, or creative impulses that don't reinforce the current power structure, they are censored.

Operating in this type of environment doesn't just impact your resumé, it influences your sense of self and the priorities that shape your character.

Regardless of the personal values we bring to any group, if we work long enough in an environment that operates according to the Big Ship rules, our values will be affected. To some extent, we internalize the values of any group we associate with for a prolonged period. This is natural in a situation where we feel pressure to rationalize behavior we don't generally approve of or admire in order to fit in. This has been the case for many of my clients who have operated in Big Ship cultures for a long time.

In no particular order, here are four negative tendencies that clients feel they have been conditioned to normalize by working in a Big Ship culture. Some of these may resonate with you more than others — and you may have experienced others that aren't on this list. In addition to evaluating the behavior of your company's leaders, use this list to evaluate your own behavior. If you find yourself embodying any of these tendencies associated with the Big Ship mindset, this is another sign to ready your lifeboat.

1.   Your words and actions don't need to align as long as you maintain an image that pleases the people in power; what you say often matters more than what you do.
2.   You focus on maintaining a superficially polite image, but you don't get too close to anyone personally.
3.   You get the maximum production out of people and don't worry about the human cost of accomplishing this.
4.   You ignore problems for as long as possible and, if they persist, make sure you don't get blamed.

## The Lifeboat Shift Starts from Within

Everyone pays lip service to the concept that people matter. However, in high-stress cultures, the importance of others at a human level can become an abstract idea that's ignored or shoved aside when it's inconvenient. Relationships can become expendable, communication can feel tedious, and frank feedback can seem like a mythic concept.

That unfortunate attitude is one of many reasons that the lessons embedded within the story of the *Titanic* are so vital for our lives and careers today.

When Captain Smith and Major Butt were working together to get as many people into lifeboats as possible, their commitment to the value of human life wasn't conceptual — it was heroic. What's more, once those same people who had been helped off the *Titanic* found themselves watching the giant ship disappear beneath the surface of the ocean, there was nothing abstract about the importance of human life.

On each lifeboat, as people huddled together in the dark trying to stay warm and reach help, each person's rank or background didn't matter — nor do yours in a lifeboat situation. It's you, your attitude, and an oar that make the difference. As you move through this process, you will see that your attitude may be what saves you!

Ultimately, once the ship hits an iceberg — the crisis has begun. Whether you're on a cruise ship in the middle of the Atlantic Ocean or in an organization grappling with an unexpected financial crisis, at this point you can't change the external challenge. You have to face it. By this point, managing your inner iceberg becomes paramount. Otherwise, you risk being overwhelmed by despair, unsure what to do, unable to act, and sitting silently waiting for orders from Big Ship leaders who may have abandoned you.

To make the decision to get into a lifeboat, and to survive once you're in one, requires honoring and accessing your own personal authority (which I discuss further in the next two chapters). You must trust yourself to know when to act and then muster the strength and courage to do so, while also helping and leading others as necessary.

## LIFEBOAT CASE STUDY
### Peter Makes a Sea Change

Peter, a senior executive for a large financial services firm, was notoriously abrasive. His saving grace was that he knew this about himself.

"I'm hiring you to work with three of my most fantastic people," he told me bluntly when his firm retained me as an executive coach. "I'm a jerk under pressure, and your job is to make sure they know I appreciate them so they don't quit when I have a bad day."

I didn't see much of Peter after that.

The three people he had hired me to work with met with me regularly. While they often needed to blow off steam due to Peter's penchant for public temper tantrums, they simultaneously revered his keen investment instincts. The firm was making money, and everyone felt pretty good.

Then this firm hit its "iceberg." The subprime mortgage crisis brought them to their knees.

The day after the firm's stock price plummeted, I got a phone call from Peter asking me to meet him for breakfast. I hadn't seen the man in months and was, to put it mildly, surprised.

Seeing this normally confident and imposing man while his firm's stock was in the midst of a fire sale was a life lesson on many levels. He asked to meet at a quiet restaurant near Grand Central Station in New York, and he got there before I did. This was notable because the employees I was coaching complained that he was notorious for keeping people waiting.

The minute I sat down, Peter got straight to the point.

"I've asked you here because I want to help my people," Peter said shakily. "These men and women have trusted their futures and the futures of their families to me — and I feel like our firm has failed them." At this point, words failed him because he teared up and couldn't speak again until we had both paused long enough for the enormity of the situation to settle the emotional energy between us.

Then we talked about practical actions he could take — providing references, lifelines, and when necessary, his personal financial support for members of his team. In some cases, the people he wanted to support were staff members who had judged him to be inconsiderate and self-serving in the past due to his brash interpersonal demeanor.

During the course of that breakfast, Peter told me that he had been reviewing the latest in a series of feedback surveys his firm had conducted to try to keep the organization on track.

"We really lost our way," Peter lamented as he described how several members of the management committee had invested in expensive feedback surveys that ended up confirming their competing biases rather than stimulating the type of fresh thinking necessary to help the firm survive.

"The crux of the matter was that no matter who was collecting data or why, the whole process was steeped in fear. As you know, useless feedback makes me crazy," he confessed.

I did know. My clients had shared with me his penchant for railing about the endless brainstorming sessions he was asked to attend when there was little accountability for how any of these discussions were going to translate into productive action. In other words, the company was in the grip of a Big Ship mindset that kept them from responding effectively to danger. While Peter had recognized this as a problem a year before the firm went under, he hadn't done anything to change their approach.

Then, Peter stunned me.

He pulled out notes he had made from the one discussion we had had about how other people might feel about themselves after spending time in his presence. Apparently, he jotted those notes down for himself the day that he met me — which was also the day he had hired me to work with three of his direct reports.

During the course of our breakfast, Peter made a commitment to have conversations with all of his directs to make sure each and every one understood how much he had valued working with them. What's more, he started making notes to put together an action plan to back up his words of encouragement with actionable support.

Sometimes you don't know who people are until the stakes get high enough.

Sometimes, when the stakes get high enough, people discover their true leadership potential.

That's what happened to Peter.

At some point during our discussion, Peter and I got onto the topic of how vital it is to create an environment of trust, so that employees feel safe enough to provide frank feedback under pressure (which breaks the Big Ship rules).

"If I could turn back time," Peter lamented, "I would have pulled back from the emotional drama playing out in my own department to consider the bigger picture at our firm more objectively. I would have taken the time to have more thoughtful conversations with people. I would have listened. I simply had no idea that losing my temper publicly, not to mention berating my colleagues harshly, was contributing to a climate where our whole firm — and our shareholders — would end up paying the price!"

Peter knew that feedback mattered. What he and his firm learned the hard way was that feedback matters most when it comes to managing the very resources that are toughest to quantify but vital for professional survival: loyalty, motivation, and trust.

When leaders like Peter are willing to transcend their personal biases and demonstrate emotional agility, they have made the

Lifeboat shift. At this point, they bring more than intellectual brilliance to problem solving; they bring wisdom.

Roughly a year later, Peter asked me to meet him for lunch. He was starting a new firm, he had the backing of seed investors he trusted, and he was determined to create a culture where the talent he hired felt respected and motivated.

After he'd been in business for six months, Peter hired me to do a series of brief feedback meetings with his new staff so he could get a sense of how he was coming across as a leader.

Since Peter knew I would give him bad news as well as good, I figured he'd be delighted by the glowing feedback he was getting from his new team. They found him thoughtful, respectful...even humble. Was this the same guy!?

I was struck by how somber Peter looked when I went through the feedback with him. "I can't figure out why you aren't happier about this," I told him. "Your team seems so positive — why aren't you?"

"I don't want to backslide," Peter told me sadly. "I don't want to get complacent and risk losing my temper and bullying people again."

"Nobody's perfect," I reassured him. "We all lose it sometimes. It's the capacity to repair — and the willingness to look at ourselves with compassion and humor — that keeps us all on track."

"What's the main thing I'm doing differently this time?" Peter asked me.

"Peter," I told him confidently, "because you have learned to be mindful of how your thoughts and feelings work together, you are a man who has mastered the art of pausing."

As he took this feedback in, I finally saw him smile.

*Lifeboat Question #4*

# WHAT IF I FREEZE IN A CRISIS?

The drama that enveloped everyone aboard the *Titanic* after the ship hit the iceberg begs a simple question: *When an unexpected challenge presents itself, how will I react?*

Do you know the answer? In fact, one lesson of the *Titanic* is that we can't know until the unexpected actually arrives.

There wasn't a soul on the *Titanic* that night prepared for the magnitude of the tragedy that engulfed them. Every individual was caught off guard and facing death. Everyone was forced to confront their most primal fears — and how they reacted reflected their sense of self, their values, their expectations of others, and their overall capacity to adapt effectively under pressure.

The sinking of the *Titanic* shocked the public and dominated headlines around the world. Everyone had questions. An official inquiry into what went wrong was promptly held by the British Board of Trade. Safety precautions were debated: about respecting iceberg warnings, having enough lifeboats, conducting regular drills, and so on. As far as the behavior of Captain Smith and the crew was concerned, the main criticism was that the ship was traveling too fast during treacherous conditions. While regulations concerning speed requirements were discussed, what wasn't scrutinized in exploring *why* the ship hadn't slowed down or been more cautious was the thought process of those in charge.

How mentally prepared was the crew for the unexpected? In spite of their years at sea, were the crew members encouraged to exercise their best personal judgment in a crisis? Were personnel, who were entrusted with the safety of others, encouraged to take initiative, solve problems, and respond with agility when facing the unknown?

Emergency procedures are important, but they pale next to mental preparation and inner strength. We can't anticipate every threat, and sometimes, threats force us to respond in unplanned ways — in ways that break the rules or that we aren't trained for. As the *Titanic* story makes clear, if people become overwhelmed in a crisis and are unable to cope with their emotions, they may freeze at just the moment they need to focus. They crash into an "inner iceberg" of fear, panic, and self-doubt, and then act in ways that are ineffective or only make things worse.

Not everyone on the *Titanic* reacted this way, and in this and the next three chapters, I shift to focus on the interpersonal dynamics that played out among the passengers on Lifeboat #6 after the ocean liner sank. How did these people respond to one another when they were thrown together in a sink-or-swim situation? Did they react predictably, given what we know of them? Who unexpectedly rose to meet the challenges, and who fell apart?

These lifeboat passengers were in a daunting situation. Everything they had counted on to keep them safe had been stripped away. They were isolated, vulnerable, and just plain scared. Most of all, no one was going to survive the night if they didn't pull together.

How did they do it? Ultimately, the relational dynamics that played out on Lifeboat #6 illustrate the critical importance of cultivating one's mental strength and personal authority. Everyone experiences fear in a crisis and needs to work with others they can trust and rely on to survive. The keys are maintaining composure under pressure and, through informal leadership, fostering the kind of group effort that helps everyone. Examining how people on Lifeboat #6 handled the tension and stress of survival can help us learn how to prepare ourselves to do these things whenever a crisis hits our workplace or threatens our career.

In this chapter, I look at the freeze response, and the person who illustrates this most vividly is Quartermaster Robert Hichens. Hichens almost literally "froze at the wheel" when *Titanic* crashed, and he froze again in Lifeboat #6. This was not how he wanted to act or how his superiors expected him to respond, and we can learn from his mistakes.

## Robert Hichens: Frozen in Fear

In the midst of chaos while the lifeboats were being loaded, Second Officer Lightoller ordered Hichens to take charge of the passengers being loaded onto Lifeboat #6 and lead them to safety. Hichens was a trained British seaman with over fourteen years of experience. Based on his credentials, he seemed like a straightforward choice for the job.

Sadly, despite all his maritime experience and training, Hichens was clearly unprepared mentally and emotionally for the challenges he would face on Lifeboat #6.

Of course, everyone on that lifeboat was afraid — some were terrified. The evacuation became increasingly chaotic as the lifeboats were being filled and lowered. From what we know, Hichens assisted with the boarding of Lifeboat #6 without incident. Presumably,

Hichens gave Lightoller no reason to second-guess putting him in charge. Everyone was trying to rise to the occasion, and surely Hichens could be trusted to lead this lifeboat to safety.

That didn't happen.

Once Lifeboat #6 pushed away from *Titanic*, Hichens basically froze. This surprised everyone. It may have even surprised Hichens — who knows?

What we *do* know from firsthand accounts is that instead of keeping people's spirits up and taking constructive action, Hichens sat rigidly in the stern babbling on about how there was little to no chance of survival without a compass or a chart, and so on.

When Arthur Peuchen, a personal friend of Captain Smith who had been traveling in first class, asked Hichens to help row, Hichens refused. When he was asked to turn back and help other passengers struggling in the water, Hichens balked. In fact, when he was asked just about anything, Hichens was surly and argumentative, and he kept reciting a litany of discouraging facts, as if he was trying to convince everyone that they were doomed.

Why couldn't Hichens carry on? Why did he freeze? The answer provides important lessons for us all.

Naturally, when I begged for the *Titanic* story to be read at bedtime during my childhood, I never imagined myself reacting like Hichens. I imagined being a hero. But as much as I hate to admit it, I've learned that it's hard to be one's best under pressure. When I'm honest with myself, I have to admit that I haven't always acted heroically in my own life. For instance, when I was working as a portfolio manager, I can recall tough days in the market when I retreated to my office, feeling lost and unsure what to do. On those dark days when I was feeling exhausted and anxious, I snapped at coworkers and drove them away. Sure, I apologized quickly, but the damage was done.

Today, I feel compassion for Hichens that I never felt as a child. Now I know that we all freeze at some point in our lives. Everyone hits an inner iceberg eventually. Depending upon the situation, this can be unavoidable. Unexpected challenges arise when we aren't ready, and at times these events can sink us emotionally, driving us into despair and passivity. The challenge is learning how to cope better the next time, and that's how Hichens's story can help.

Who was Robert Hichens? He was a regular person, like any of us. First of all, Hichens really needed the job he got on the *Titanic*. A husband and father, Hichens was finding it tough to support his family as a seaman. Because of the coal miners' strike prior to the *Titanic*'s maiden voyage, many Atlantic crossings had been canceled; it was a tight job market. The competition to get a place on the *Titanic*'s crew was fierce, and men and women who had been out of work for weeks were physically jostling for positions in line to be considered.

When Hichens found out that he was confirmed as a quartermaster on *Titanic*, he was both elated and relieved. This was going to be the most prestigious post he had held in the course of his career. It also meant he could feed his family.

I don't think it's a stretch to assume that Hichens was highly motivated to do the best job he possibly could. As he lined up with the nine hundred other members of the smartly attired *Titanic* crew for inspection by Captain Smith, Hichens didn't just have a job — he had an admirable place in the world that gave him a sense of identity.

One of his professional responsibilities was delivering messages throughout this massive ship. Hichens would head deep down into the engine room of the *Titanic* and then make the trek back up to the bridge of the ship. As he did this, Hichens observed two distinctly different worlds. The men doing the backbreaking work of making sure the coal burned properly worked tirelessly underneath first-class passengers expecting to enjoy a calm and luxurious voyage. The internal distance between the haves and have-nots on that voyage rivaled the size of the ocean they were crossing.

This was the most important job Hichens had ever had in his life. He took it seriously and was committed to following navigational orders from officers on the bridge with precision. In fact, once he got an order, Hichens was trained to repeat it back exactly to demonstrate that he had clearly heard and understood the command.

On the cold Sunday night of *Titanic*'s sinking, Hichens was at the helm in the wheelhouse, and thanks to the drastic drop in the temperature, just about everyone else who could justify crawling into a warm bed had done so. What's more, as I describe in chapter 2 ("Danger on the Horizon," pages 54–59), there was a brief period when the two men assigned to stand watch with Hichens in the wheelhouse — Fourth Officer Boxhall and Sixth Officer Moody — both dashed out briefly at the same time. One of these junior officers should have stayed in the wheelhouse, and looking back, this failure was catastrophic.

Hichens wasn't in any position to question their timing or their judgment. Officers Boxhall and Moody had served together on the *Oceanic*, another ship from White Star Line. Not only was Hichens outranked, he was the "new guy."

The same went for First Officer Murdoch, who was in command on this shift. Murdoch had served as the first officer alongside Captain Smith on the *Titanic*'s sister ship, *Olympic*, and he was one of the most well-respected officers of the White Star Line. Nobody questioned Murdoch's authority, much less where he chose to position himself during a shift, even if standing on the bridge that evening put him out of earshot and out of sight of Hichens.

Thus, Hichens was truly alone in the wheelhouse holding the ship steady when he heard Frederick Fleet ring the bell three times from the crow's nest. Hichens knew what this meant — an iceberg had been spotted. Trapped in one of history's worst no-win situations, Hichens couldn't act on his own without committing an unimaginable breach of discipline. He wasn't authorized to take his hands off the wheel, change course, or take any other type of individual initiative.

One can only imagine how long every second felt for Robert Hichens as he waited for his superior officers to respond to Fleet's warning. Did he ponder the number of people whose lives depended upon what he did next? Was he angry about being left in this predicament? Did he trust the judgment of the ship's officers? Did he still believe the ship was unsinkable?

When Murdoch *finally* yelled out the order to change course, Hichens responded immediately. This was the command he'd been waiting for. By this point, Moody and Boxhall had both dashed back to the wheelhouse. Feet anchored to the ground, Hichens repeated Murdoch's order as he turned the wheel with all his might.

For a few precious seconds, everyone among the crew held their breath hoping that the ship had turned in time. That glimmer of hope was dashed as the iceberg moved along *Titanic*'s starboard bow. After that grim scrape, the next sound Hichens remembered hearing was the bell signaling the engine room to close the watertight doors.

What thoughts raced through Hichens's mind after this? What might any of us have thought? No doubt, we'd fear being blamed for this tragedy. We would be asking ourselves: *Was it my fault? What do I do now? Will anyone ever hire me again? What about my family? Is there anything I could have done differently?*

This may help explain Hichens's behavior in Lifeboat #6. He didn't freeze because he didn't know how to handle a vessel in the ocean, nor even because he feared dying. Hichens was likely replaying those final moments before impact and feeling emotionally paralyzed by the part he had played in the nightmare now engulfing everyone. When the *Titanic* hit the iceberg, he was at the wheel, and that's all anyone might remember. Even if he lived, his future was ruined.

Of course, we can't know precisely what Hichens thought, but his situation embodies a conflict that people often face in a crisis: Do they act without authority in whatever way seems necessary, or do they obediently play whatever role they have been assigned? Hichens was trained as a seaman, which meant he had to wait for orders from a superior officer before acting. He had stuck to his Big Ship script, and that had led to tragedy.

Under normal circumstances, waiting for orders was the right thing to do. But in an instant, circumstances weren't normal, and even though his every instinct must have been screaming to do *something*, Hichens wasn't able to give himself the personal authority to act.

The crushing emotional burden of that mistake was the "inner iceberg" that may have caused Hichens to freeze under pressure on Lifeboat #6. Ironically, he was put in charge of the lifeboat; he now had the authority to give orders that he'd lacked before. But the cumulative weight of the despair, shame, guilt, and fear of having played a part in the tragedy that had destroyed *Titanic* was no doubt too much to bear. He gave up, abdicating his responsibility.

In our lives and careers, it's easy to see this same dynamic at play, though with less dire results. Anyone who has ever felt distracted on the job by an inner pileup of dark feelings and discouraging thoughts has hit an inner iceberg. If someone's mental energy is caught up speculating about what might go wrong next, they will find themselves more physically exhausted, less alert, and more prone to freeze or overreact unproductively at just the moment that peak performance is needed.

These inner icebergs grow beneath the surface of our every-day consciousness. Most of us don't want to pay attention to the buildup of troubling thoughts and emotions that feed our inner iceberg. Acknowledging difficult emotions that are at odds with our self-image is hard. We all want to believe we will perform well and stay positive under pressure.

However, ignoring what's building up in our inner worlds isn't the way to navigate inner icebergs; that only ensures we hit them.

## When the Big Ship Mindset Hits an Inner Iceberg

To clarify what "freezing" under pressure means on the job, this is a physical, emotional, and mental reaction to any upsetting situation. What happens is that, as the person tries to suppress the unwanted feelings or thoughts, their body gets tense, their awareness narrows, and their behavior tends to shift into autopilot.

However, the response people have to suppressed feelings can unfold differently for different people and in different situations. Some people freeze, like Hichens; others lash out; and still others display a combination of extreme reactions as they strive to avoid uncomfortable feelings under stress. Are you aware of what happens to you? Do you talk over others in high-pressure meetings? Do you clamp your mouth shut rather than speak a difficult truth? Do you isolate from others and focus on distractions, such as overeating, overspending, or binge-watching television?

How we respond to unexpected challenges has a lot to do with our expectations. The *Titanic* is a clear example of the false expectations cultivated by the Big Ship mindset, which fosters self-defeating responses to problems. The captain and crew of the *Titanic*, believing their ship unsinkable, didn't believe an iceberg could cause them any real damage. This belief in their invincibility prompted them to disregard the iceberg warnings they received and minimize the precautions necessary to avoid danger. The senior officers on the *Titanic* didn't conduct safety drills, practice emergency procedures with the crew, or empower subordinates, like Hichens, to take initiative in a crisis.

In hindsight, this Big Ship mindset posed the real risk to the *Titanic*. If they'd sailed with a Lifeboat mindset, they would have heeded all warnings, slowed down, adjusted course, prepared and empowered the crew, and likely avoided tragedy.

With all this in mind, let's consider what we can learn from Hichens about facing our own inner iceberg.

Like Hichens, we all have moments when we have to face our inner iceberg. Doing this is particularly challenging when we have spent years working in a culture where the Big Ship mindset rules. Almost all my clients with experience in Big Ship cultures report becoming gradually conditioned to suppress their feelings and to play their assigned role in an organization.

Yet to manage an inner iceberg effectively, we have to be able to identify our feelings without judging ourselves harshly. This isn't about looking strong — it's about genuinely being strong from the inside out. We can't be strong on the job, or anywhere else for that matter, if we aren't allowed to feel. Trying not to feel is what prevents us from being able to respond to a crisis effectively, and it can prompt us to behave in self-sabotaging ways under pressure.

Hichens didn't freeze because of his feelings, per se. Hichens froze because he was channeling all of his energy into avoiding them.

To prepare yourself to respond effectively under pressure, it's vital to understand the progression of thoughts and feelings that unfold in your inner world when you hit an inner iceberg. While avoiding what's happening in your inner world may seem easier in the short term, it stunts the emotional agility you need to cultivate to keep your career on track.

By acknowledging your feelings and embracing them as a source of wisdom, you learn the vital skill of aligning your emotional and mental energy in a manner that strengthens your ability to think clearly, trust your own judgment, and adapt under pressure.

## Four Stages of a Big Ship Reaction

What does it look and feel like when someone who has internalized and normalized the Big Ship mindset meets an inner iceberg?

Here's a quick synopsis of the four stages of this reaction:

1. **An unexpected challenge emerges**, and this triggers some combination of anxiety, fear, self-doubt, and uncertainty.
2. **Difficult feelings are suppressed**, especially if they don't fit our assigned or expected role, or if they point toward an unorthodox course of action.
3. **A story is created that justifies the reaction.** Rather than admitting and validating these feelings, we create a story that dismisses or denies them. For instance, we might blame others or the situation, casting ourselves as the "victim" and others as the "villain." Or we may simply rationalize our reaction as normal or not important.
4. **We freeze or overreact**; we refuse to act; we hide, distract ourselves, blow up, or stick to "safe" routines out of fear.

Let's take a closer look at each stage of this inner progression and consider how this may apply to your life and career.

### 1: An Unexpected Challenge Emerges

Life is full of the unexpected: Maybe you are losing your job because your firm is downsizing. Maybe your spouse is losing their job. Whatever it is, any potentially life-changing problem can trigger your emotions, so that you hit your inner iceberg precisely at the moment when you need to be focused, decisive, and proactive.

Hitting your inner iceberg means you are suddenly grappling with two problems: one in your inner world and one in your outer world. In truth, you need to cope with the inner problem first, since otherwise you are likely to freeze or panic and be unable to manage the external problem.

As we saw with Robert Hichens, by the time Lifeboat #6 was on its own in the Atlantic, his role as one of *Titanic*'s officers had completely fallen apart. When he hit his inner iceberg, Hichens devolved to a state where he was unable to be present in the moment and interact effectively with his fellow passengers. Even though everyone was crowded and cramped in that small boat, Hichens acted isolated and alone, and he drove others away.

To avoid freezing like Hichens, when problems arise, it's important to tune in to your own internal alarm bells. Do you sense an inner iceberg, and can you cope with the anxiety it evokes before you crash into it?

### 2: Difficult Feelings Are Suppressed

It's hard to put things in perspective when you are cut off from your feelings. Feelings can switch channels fast — so that memories, worries, and regrets can fill your mind quickly. No matter how intelligent or well-trained you are, when suppressed feelings start flooding your inner world, it's easy to lose sight of what's most important in the present moment. When people are under pressure, adrenaline courses through their bodies, and a self-reinforcing vortex of negative thoughts and feelings can transform them into someone they barely recognize.

This is why, as opposed to freezing, some people explode when they hit an inner iceberg. If someone feels too much internal pressure, if the emotions are too much to contain, then those emotions break through, much like a pressure cooker lets off steam. You got it — anger is often the only note on the keyboard that can drown out the other feelings we don't want to face.

### 3: A Story Is Created That Justifies the Reaction

In a crisis, if we hit an inner iceberg and find ourselves reacting in ways we know aren't heroic — that don't help others, that don't solve the problem, that don't reflect who we want to be — then we have a choice: admit to feeling vulnerable, overwhelmed, and needing help, or create a story that justifies our reaction.

That's what Robert Hichens did. He argued that they were all doomed and that nothing they could do would save them. He told the other lifeboat passengers that they didn't understand the risks of being in a small boat in the middle of the ocean as well as he did. A storm could blow them to bits. The suction of the *Titanic* going under could take them all down. According to the story Hichens was creating, rowing was useless, so why even try?

People who have internalized the norms of the Big Ship mindset create stories as well. Rather than act in effective ways, they may blame others, dwell on the past, cast themselves as a victim — anything they can *possibly* think up to avoid the present moment will do. Why? In part because they don't fully trust themselves. They feel vulnerable. If they've been conditioned to operate from a script, to play only one role, then they may feel incapable of playing other roles or being able to handle facing the unknown.

Of course, if you can't face the facts, you can't improve the situation. This is how many people get stuck.

Like Hichens, the more someone creates a story in order to justify themselves, the more isolated they become from others. Hichens lost the confidence of his fellow passengers, and command of the group, because neither his actions nor his story were helpful. Others in the lifeboat refused to accept his story, and soon enough they turned to another person to manage the group and help them survive.

### 4: We Freeze or Overreact

Once someone has proceeded through the first three stages, they will likely wind up here: freezing when action is needed, acting out unproductively, or proceeding like it's business as usual while a crisis looms. These responses, or any combination of them, will prove to be inadequate, inappropriate, unhelpful. Further, the inability to respond authentically in the moment can lead to a breakdown of the self that can have personal as well as professional consequences.

In other words, when people operate from the Big Ship mindset in a crisis, they tend to make the situation worse, which becomes frustrating for everyone involved. That's what happened to Hichens on Lifeboat #6. Not only did Arthur Peuchen argue with Hichens, but Margaret Brown spoke up, shut him down fast, and started taking action to help her fellow passengers. This soon led to a power struggle, since Hichens, despite his inaction, did not want to relinquish the authority of his role. This part of the story is what I discuss in the next chapter, but here's a spoiler: The group sided with Brown.

When I tell people that you can have a good career if you're smart, but you will only have a great career if you're brave, it's because facing your inner iceberg takes courage.

Cultivating that courage is crucial if you don't want to go down with the ship!

## Practice Emergency Procedures
## Before Disaster Strikes

Nobody intends to break down in an emergency, to freeze under pressure and fail to help when people need help the most.

Not even Hichens.

Sadly, this can happen to anyone if we neglect our inner world. Having worked with a wide range of ambitious professionals, I'm used to being around people who take their physical self-care seriously. It's not uncommon for my clients to hit the gym on a regular basis, most of them eat pretty well, and many of them do their best to dress stylishly, drive nice cars, and live in well-maintained homes.

When it comes to the inner stuff, however, self-care can become neglected. People may start by cutting corners in little ways, like jumping up from family meals to take a call or return an office email. Then they find themselves working on vacation and unable to sleep from anxiety, so they get up in the middle of the night to keep working or check their social media accounts — which they rationalize as no big deal. Everybody does it.

If they are working in an environment where overscheduling and constant pressure are "business as usual," then suppressing feelings becomes normalized and their inner iceberg just keeps getting bigger.

In order to avoid this, we need to practice making the Lifeboat shift ahead of time, or rather, all the time. Metaphorically, we need to regularly practice the emergency procedures we'll need in a crisis, so we are familiar with how to ready the lifeboats and row to safety. We need to recondition ourselves to "check in" emotionally and spot internal signals of trouble before a crisis hits. These signs can be as subtle as a fleeting feeling or as blatant as a painful headache. Yet these clues alert us to problems in the present moment, which we can then assess and handle before our inner iceberg becomes unmanageable. That helps keep our lives and careers on track.

As I say, Hichens was trained to handle watercraft. He knew how to work with ropes, how to row, and how to maintain the boat's balance on the open ocean. What he lacked was the training to handle his emotions under pressure, and this turned out to be even more important.

In other words, it's vital to take the safety precautions necessary to maintain your inner resilience before the unexpected occurs. In the same way you eat well and work out, keep yourself in good emotional shape every day.

## LIFEBOAT CASE STUDY, PART 1
### Marie's Emotional Agility Is Tested

Marie, a marketing consultant, started the Lifeboat Process when the challenge of working with an important client at her new firm proved to be far larger than she had anticipated.

Marie had always considered herself to be a positive and solution-oriented professional. She prided herself on her ability to keep her boss, her staff, and her clients happy. The problem was that she tended to be more positive with others than she was with herself — particularly under pressure.

A single mother of two, Marie was so eager to sign on the dotted line when she was offered a new leadership position that her hands actually shook as she sealed the deal. Because her heart was racing in eager anticipation, Marie barely listened when her new boss alluded to the fact that Nancy, the most important client that Marie would inherit from her predecessor, was considered "difficult."

Marie was so focused on impressing her new boss with her credentials that she didn't pause to consider how the simultaneous demands of onboarding at a new firm, helping her kids matriculate into a new school system, and integrating into a new community as a single parent might tax her inner resources.

Why didn't Marie assess these challenges more thoughtfully? As a seasoned professional, she would have quickly spotted these risks in a prospective hire! Why did she work so hard to downplay these risks when it came to the support she would need to succeed in this new role?

Like many of us, Marie had conditioned herself to minimize things that didn't fit the expectations of the role she had scripted for herself, which exemplifies Big Ship thinking at its finest.

Confident that she could win over any "difficult" client with hard work and a positive attitude, Marie's expectations of how this situation would unfold were colored by her conviction that, no matter what, she could count on herself to handle it.

Needless to say, all those expectations became part of the problem. Let's examine Marie's story through the stages of a Big Ship reaction.

## 1: An Unexpected Challenge Emerges

Like many Big Ship thinkers, Marie felt invulnerable. She never anticipated a client who might be difficult enough to sink her self-image.

Three months into her new job, with her house on the market and her kids entering a new school system, Marie felt like tearing her hair out. Nancy, the "difficult" client, was driving her nuts.

Referring to Nancy as "difficult" proved to be an understatement worthy of the driest British humor.

Nancy's account represented millions of dollars of revenue to

Marie's firm, and Nancy knew it. Nancy proved to be a master of detail — particularly the types of details that put Marie and her team on edge and left everybody reeling emotionally.

Marie's hopes that her interpersonal charm would save the day were quickly dashed.

Nancy questioned everything. She questioned the firm's billing practices, the nuances of the latest statement of work, the work ethic of Marie and her team, and even the expense reports of junior staff members. When Marie tried to address thorny issues with Nancy directly, Nancy reacted by shooting off emails to Marie's boss that accused the whole department of covering up contract breaches and inappropriate billing practices.

The more Nancy criticized, the more powerless Marie felt. This was a sign Marie had crashed right into her inner iceberg.

## 2: Difficult Feelings Are Suppressed

Marie was familiar with the concept of emotional intelligence. In fact, in the course of her career, Marie had consistently invested in training programs for her staff that stressed emotional honesty and the value of teamwork.

The problem was that, under pressure, Marie wasn't able to apply what she knew about emotional intelligence to her relationship with herself. Remember, thinking about skills like pausing or being mindful of what's happening in our minds and bodies is different from actually putting this knowledge into practice.

Caught up in the Big Ship mindset, Marie believed that strength meant speed. Rather than pausing to assess when Nancy lashed out at her team, Marie found herself thinking faster, reacting hastily, and setting a tone with her team that normalized a pervasive sense of urgency. The frantic pace Marie was setting undermined her ability to listen strategically — both to herself and to others.

When members of her team came in for guidance, Marie was too distracted to focus thoughtfully on what they were trying to tell her. Marie's management style became increasingly chaotic and unfocused, and two key members of her department, who had been considering resigning, left abruptly.

Marie was mortified. Her boss wasn't pleased either.

Things weren't much better on the home front. By the end of the day, Marie was testy. Her kids had stopped sharing their personal concerns with her for fear of adding to the pent-up frustration she seemed to be dragging home from the office.

### 3: A Story Is Created That Justifies the Reaction

Marie needed a narrative to explain her failures and to keep herself going. The one she created was that Nancy was a terrible person who was simply impossible to please!

In other words, Marie decided to blame the iceberg for the fact that she ran into it. Although the real problem was the Big Ship mindset that kept her from adapting and changing course, Marie didn't realize this yet. The simple truth is that we can't control the outer challenges we face. Sometimes, there's no avoiding trouble. But ultimately, the way we deploy our inner resources is what will sink our ship or save the day.

By "blaming the iceberg," Marie cast herself as the victim of a tragic drama. She felt sorry for herself, and her mind whirled with resentment and a sense of helplessness. Why wasn't her boss standing up for her? Why were members of her team looking for other jobs? Didn't they realize how hard she was working to save their careers? Why were her kids shutting her out? Didn't they realize that she was doing all of this for them!?

As exhaustion, resentment, and fear got the better of her, Marie started to despair. As her inner iceberg grew, her perspective on the situation shrank. By this point, she could only envision two potential outcomes: She would either totally succeed or completely fail.

## 4: Marie Freezes or Overreacts

Marie felt trapped and overwhelmed and decided to give up. Prior to starting the Lifeboat Process, Marie told me her plan was to march into her boss's office, trash-talk Nancy, and quit, telling her boss that he would never keep anyone in her role until he learned to be more supportive. That would show everyone!

I asked Marie if she had a backup plan for her career, and the defiant gleam in her eye faded. Upon reflection, she admitted that what she wanted to change wasn't her job — it was the way she was reacting to it.

When clients like Marie share professional struggles that tempt them to resign impulsively, I always remind them that you can't solve life's challenges and make strategic decisions until you master your inner world. When people are driven by fear, they sometimes risk leaving a job without a backup plan to avoid tackling their inner iceberg.

Fortunately, Marie got the message, as well as a chance to course-correct.

*Lifeboat Question #5*

# HOW DO I FIND INNER STRENGTH UNDER PRESSURE?

The passengers on Lifeboat #6 were huddled together in horror as they witnessed something unthinkable. Suddenly, the stern of their "ship of dreams" rose into the air as the forward half of the *Titanic* began to sink. Then, the forward funnel of the ship toppled toward the bow, and people began to slide off of the ship's deck into the freezing water below.

The subsequent screams and sounds of tearing metal preceded a shocking finale. First, the lights on the ship went out. Then, as the ship split between the third and fourth funnels, the bow of the ship slid below the surface and the stern rose until it was almost perpendicular in the water. Finally, after remaining vertical and motionless for what must have felt like an eternity, the *Titanic* plunged beneath the surface of the ocean.

Within moments, it was gone.

By this point, the passengers on Lifeboat #6 weren't just on a different boat; they were in a different reality. In this new reality, the external symbols of social status and rank were no longer priorities. The new priority was survival.

Everything had changed.

We explored Robert Hichens's reaction to this situation in the last chapter. At precisely the moment that courage was needed, Hichens found himself floundering emotionally, isolated from his fellow passengers, and unable to lead. From Hichens's perspective, all was lost.

But not everyone reacted this way. I've always wondered what private conversations took place between the passengers on Lifeboat #6 during these terrifying moments. How would any of us respond? Did the passengers try to reassure one another? Did they pray together for their loved ones? What we know from eyewitness accounts is that, even though Hichens lost hope, many of the other passengers didn't. Others were determined to greet the next sunrise and hold their loved ones again. They weren't sure how or what to do, but as a group, they became united by their desire to survive.

This collective willingness to pull together to beat the odds produced a new perspective, what I call the Lifeboat mindset. This mindset values survival over status; it regards group effort as essential to individual survival; and it values every person. Everyone deserved to be saved, and everyone's effort was needed. As the Lifeboat mindset spread from passenger to passenger, an informal leader emerged who gave their priorities a voice. That leader was Margaret Brown.

In this chapter, I examine Brown's actions and what they can teach us about accessing our inner resources under pressure, fostering the collective strength of a group, and identifying effective action in a crisis. These lessons demonstrate how to make the Lifeboat shift so we can successfully navigate unexpected challenges in our lives and work.

## Margaret Brown: Inner Strength Under Pressure

On Lifeboat #6, as Robert Hichens froze in despair, this created a leadership vacuum that might have been catastrophic.

It almost proved to be.

An emotionally tense power struggle broke out between Hichens and Arthur Peuchen, whose friend, Captain Smith, had just gone down with the ship. Peuchen unleashed the full fury of his feelings, grief, and experience to get Hichens into line. Hichens needed to lead or defer to someone who would!

According to survivor accounts, Hichens and Peuchen fought with each other over who should have the authority to lead the group. Hichens was unwilling to pass the baton, and Peuchen felt that, as a military officer, seaman, and friend of Smith, he was the logical next choice. Yet as these two men argued over status, hierarchy, and what to do (which I describe further in the next chapter), someone else emerged who quietly took the actions necessary to unite the group and avert further tragedy: Margaret Brown.

Brown was a gracefully aging grandmother with no nautical training. Before this happened, none of the other passengers would have guessed that Brown would have been the one to save their lives. However, by the time Lifeboat #6 was rescued by the *Carpathia*, according to Logan Marshall, "Some of the passengers, in fact *all* of the women passengers of the *Titanic* who were rescued, referred to 'Lady Margaret' as the strength of them all."

What did Brown do, and how did she do it?

Margaret Brown was a first-class passenger who had bought her ticket at the last minute. In spite of the pomp and circumstance associated with this voyage, the reason this particular socialite and philanthropist had boarded the *Titanic* was that it was the first ship Brown could book passage on to visit her sick grandson.

While she had an outgoing personality, Brown was seen as

somewhat of a curiosity by many of her peers in first class. Born into humble circumstances as the daughter of a working-class Irishman, Margaret had experienced the good fortune of marrying J. J. Brown, who became an overnight millionaire when he struck gold at a Denver mine.

Further, Brown was a divorcée, which was a scandal in its own right during this era. After dissolving her marital contract with J. J. Brown, she pressed on to live her life fully as a single woman of means. Not only was Margaret a divorced woman, she was "new" money. While she dressed well and traveled frequently, her pedigree didn't exactly put her at the top of the social food chain.

However, once everyone was on Lifeboat #6 in the middle of rough seas, concerns over social distinctions were dwarfed by the need to survive. From my own experiences of boating in difficult seas with my husband, I know the physical conditions must have been terrifying. It was cold and dark, and the waves tossing those little lifeboats around must have been daunting.

Even experienced sailors struggle under these conditions. In Lifeboat #6, if Hichens refused to help, who among them had the physical strength, know-how, and courage to battle the elements and keep them afloat until, hopefully, a rescue ship arrived? Certainly not a gentle grandmother from Denver. For one thing, in 1912, women were rarely accepted as or empowered to be leaders.

But as Hichens froze, and Peuchen argued with him, Brown became focused. She somehow managed her own emotions and assessed the situation. Certainly, the outlook was grim. The Big Ship was gone and everyone else aboard *Titanic* was either in their own lifeboats or drowned. No one had yet arrived to rescue them. They were on their own. Most of these lifeboat passengers were wealthy women who normally navigated life in opulent and stylish clothing. Now they were shivering, wet, and terror-stricken.

Brown's priorities may have reinforced her resolve as well. Remember, Brown was hoping to reach the side of her gravely ill grandson. Her *Titanic* voyage was focused on the preciousness of human life. She was well aware that the will to live is one of the most powerful resources we have.

Without asking for advice or permission, Brown began to ready the oars, and she asked the women to take seats at the gunwales. Brown didn't try to convince the men to stop arguing; instead, she assessed and worked with the resources she had. Though the other women were terrified, cold, and exhausted, they agreed to do what Brown asked. Later, people aboard said that Brown did not command others, but rather she encouraged the passengers to support one another.

Unfortunately, those who tried to row found they could barely manage the heavy oars. Even though the movement of rowing at least kept them warm, they weren't getting anywhere. Margaret didn't become discouraged; she stayed present in the moment. She counted the number of oars available and the women aboard, and she realized if two women pulled each oar, they'd have sufficient strength to manage them. Indeed, with two rowers to each oar, the boat made much better progress through the water, and the mood in the lifeboat began to shift.

Ultimately, the contrast between Margaret Brown and Robert Hichens couldn't be clearer or more stark. They both faced similar icebergs — both the unexpected, real iceberg that sank *Titanic* and their inner iceberg of fear in the face of death — and each responded in opposite ways. Hichens panicked, froze, and gave up, refusing to lead even though that was his job. Brown remained calm and focused, and despite having no experience or authority, she stepped forward to lead, organizing others to work together to save themselves.

Ultimately, Brown's example also inspired both Peuchen and Fleet to make the Lifeboat shift. Perhaps this wasn't hard for Fleet, whose position as a lookout meant that his job was to stay aware of and respond to potential danger. Meanwhile, Peuchen eventually stopped wasting energy fighting with Hichens and began supporting Brown's efforts to organize the women. Like his friend Captain Smith, Peuchen was a Big Ship leader who adopted the Lifeboat mindset under pressure.

The way that the passengers on Lifeboat #6 made the Lifeboat shift has many applications in the workplace, offering lessons for dealing with our fears, interacting with others, and pulling together under pressure.

I believe the key reason that this part of the *Titanic* story made such a powerful impression on me as a child was realizing that, in order to survive this ordeal, Margaret Brown had to transcend her fear. Her strength was her emotional agility. In this book, I equate emotional agility with the ability to circumnavigate your inner iceberg under pressure. Brown found herself in an unexpected life-or-death situation that would trigger anyone's deepest fears. Yet she faced hers and didn't sink. What's more, the inner strength she embodied set a tone for the rest of the group that helped prevent them from freezing under pressure as well.

Emotional agility is a skill that anyone can cultivate. Unfortunately, this skill is often overlooked by many otherwise excellent professional training programs. Many approaches to executive education assume that intellectual instruction, carefully scripted goals, and process thinking will save the day. What the Lifeboat mindset reveals is that, without being aware of how our best thinking can be skewed by emotional triggers under pressure, we may not be able to follow the most well-intentioned advice.

Hichens had all the training necessary to navigate a lifeboat, but he crashed into his inner iceberg and never made the Lifeboat shift. Margaret Brown did.

## How the Lifeboat Mindset Navigates an Inner Iceberg

In fact, my lifelong fascination with *how* Margaret Brown responded in this crisis is what led me to develop the Lifeboat Process. The more I have explored her actions that night, the more it has taught me about how to manage difficult emotions under pressure. What's more, these lessons apply to almost any challenge we might face. These strategies help us improve both our lives and our careers.

With Margaret Brown's story in mind, let's consider what I characterize as the four stages of how someone operating from the Lifeboat mindset responds under pressure. These mirror the four stages I discuss in the previous chapter, but where a Big Ship mindset can lead us to crash into our inner iceberg, the Lifeboat mindset helps us navigate around it and act effectively.

1. **An unexpected challenge emerges.** This is some difficult event — like an accident, financial crisis, or relationship trouble — that triggers anxiety, fear, or panic. In other words, our inner iceberg.
2. **We pause to assess our thoughts and feelings.** Rather than avoid or deny our internal stress, we focus on it to identify our reaction and what it indicates or is trying to tell us.
3. **We evaluate our skills and resources in the situation.** This includes our personal skills and inner resources and the skills of anyone else involved. In other words, we ask: Who can we trust to help improve the situation?
4. Given what we discover, we **develop a plan and take action** to address the difficult event.

In contrast to the four stages that reflect the Big Ship mindset, the four steps that characterize the Lifeboat mindset tend to result in taking action to improve a situation. These actions may sometimes seem small — like Margaret Brown asking others to start rowing — but if they are practical, positive responses that address the difficulties in the present moment, they will move you in the right direction.

In short, when you make the Lifeboat shift, you don't feel powerless, you don't isolate, and you don't freeze.

Let's take a closer look at each of the four stages of the Lifeboat mindset, and how these can help you tap into your inner strengths under pressure on the job.

### 1: An Unexpected Challenge Emerges

If you are already operating from the Lifeboat mindset, then you've already learned to expect the unexpected. If you've embraced this perspective, there's a good chance you haven't stuffed a plethora of angry or depressed thoughts beneath the surface of your conscious awareness. Instead, you've made a practice of recognizing and acknowledging difficult emotions. This emotional awareness makes you better prepared to deal with any self-defeating thought patterns that might otherwise get in the way of clear-eyed judgment and awareness of the present moment.

Phew!

Even more empowering is the simple fact that you've learned to trust your own reactions under pressure. You know that ignoring or denying problems doesn't make them go away. You know that devising stories — whether to justify your behavior, to rationalize mistakes, or simply to avoid blame or consequences when things go wrong — just wastes precious time. Any Big Ship concern with appearances only distracts from the real task, which is to deal with the threat or problem facing you.

### 2: We Pause to Assess Our Thoughts and Feelings

Pausing is about assessing ourselves, almost like checking for injuries after a fender bender. If we feel afraid, what in the situation triggered that fear? What, precisely, are we most anxious about? Let's be clear: Pausing all by itself is not a magic bullet. Pausing doesn't change anything. What we do when we pause is what makes the difference. We pause to prevent ourselves from reacting in a way that makes matters worse.

Rather than freeze or risk overreacting when we face an unexpected threat, we pause in order to slow down our emotions. This helps us put our emotional response to the challenge into perspective. By pausing, we take the time to acknowledge our inner iceberg, distinguish between what we can and can't change, accept what we must face, and evaluate the widest range of positive responses available in the present moment.

Pausing also helps us use the adrenaline prompted by any crisis to widen the range of positive outcomes we can envision — rather than narrowing our focus to what can go wrong. This inner alignment brings us closer to a state where we are able to employ our intellect and intuition in concert to act effectively.

### 3: We Evaluate Our Skills and Resources

People operating from the Lifeboat mindset never forget that the ultimate goal in any crisis is to solve the problem and save as many people as possible. Remember, from the Lifeboat perspective, people matter.

Unlike Hichens, Margaret Brown didn't waste precious time lamenting their odds or the resources they lacked. She accepted that these female passengers weren't trained to row, and she realized the group's provisions on the lifeboat were minimal. However, bearing these limits in mind, Brown focused on the collective resources the group *did* have. She communicated with her fellow passengers and helped them marshal their forces.

Stage 3 is where you break the chains of isolation. From the Lifeboat perspective, the skills of others are sometimes the most precious resources in a crisis.

Big Ship thinkers who isolate under pressure aren't team players and don't delegate easily. If they are forced to build teams, many of them unconsciously strive to hire people they hope will be submissive and pliable. After all, if trust issues cause someone to view the strength of others as a challenge rather than a resource, why would they want to surround themselves with strong people?

It's important to emphasize that Brown's ability to bring out the best in others under pressure, foster trust, and unify the group stemmed from her ability to trust herself. Brown didn't let despair overwhelm her. She didn't freeze, and she didn't try to play the victim or pull rank. Brown focused on taking effective action and fostering a shared determination to survive.

## 4: We Develop a Plan and Take Action

People who operate from the Lifeboat mindset give themselves the personal authority to see what they see, use their common sense, and exercise initiative when warranted. They don't pass the buck; they take responsibility for ensuring that the task in front of them gets completed. This can be liberating because it frees people to tap into the full range of their individual strengths and to strategically combine their skills with those of others.

Have you ever noticed one of those maddening situations in a Big Ship culture where, instead of taking decisive action, a leader seems to deliberate endlessly and avoid doing anything? That is the same freeze response that afflicted Hichens, and it indicates a leader who hasn't made the Lifeboat shift.

Often, this type of managerial paralysis ensues when Big Ship thinkers are more focused on their personal image than the greater good. In fairness, this often isn't conscious. As we have seen, in a crisis, leaders can make valuable shifts and exhibit emotional agility! That said, when a pattern of repetitive meetings takes hold without any constructive action, it's often because the individuals involved are too stressed to listen strategically or too preoccupied with scoring a "big win" to prioritize the small changes that can help keep the group moving in a positive direction.

Margaret Brown realized that keeping the rest of the passengers rowing might not save the day, but it was their best bet! Everyone needed to at least keep moving to stay warm enough to survive the cold. Brown's courage and presence of mind illustrate that, when facing the unknown, the ability to trust your decision-making process and take action can be as vital as the decisions you make.

The Lifeboat mindset doesn't just help you make more strategic decisions. It fortifies your ability to trust yourself, live your truth, and take practical, positive, and powerful action — one stroke of the oar at a time.

## LIFEBOAT CASE STUDY, PART 2
### Marie Adopts the Lifeboat Mindset

At the last minute, Marie decided not to quit her job. She decided to change her attitude and approach by adopting the Lifeboat mindset to see if she could meet the challenge of her company's extremely difficult client, Nancy. Here is what she did to get her work and life back on track, which relates to the four stages of navigating your inner iceberg.

### 1: Marie Navigates an Unexpected Challenge

Even though Marie's first reaction to Nancy led her to crash into her inner iceberg — so that she became frozen in fear and ready to resign — her situation afforded her a second chance.

First, she paused to consider if resigning would be an effective action in this situation, and she quickly realized it would not. Marie hadn't been in her new position long enough to resign without putting her professional reputation, and her family's financial situation, in peril.

She also considered her inner iceberg and realized that the unrelenting pressure and the emotional inner hell she felt were things she was *putting on herself*. She was taking the client and the situation personally, and this was taking a toll on her energy level, her sense of presence, and her effectiveness in her job. This hurt her interactions with others and left her far too drained to effectively consider finding another job.

Adopting a more realistic (and less pessimistic) perspective helped Marie give herself permission to postpone the decision about resigning until she'd done the inner work necessary to strengthen her relationship with herself.

One decision made. One thing off the critical list. Whew!

In essence, working with Nancy had proved to be far more difficult than Marie had anticipated. To address this challenge effectively, Marie needed to clarify the emotional triggers she was experiencing as well as the problems that were unfolding on the job. By objectively facing this situation without overdramatizing or personalizing it, Marie was able to stop working fast — and start working smart.

### 2: Marie Pauses to Assess Her Thoughts and Feelings

As Marie paused to assess her emotions, she realized that one of the biggest challenges she faced was that she rarely took the time necessary to quietly focus on what she was feeling and evaluate why she felt that way. As a single parent and senior executive, Marie was used to doing things fast and packing as much into her schedule as possible.

Thus, learning to make a habit of pausing was her first task. Like many of my clients, Marie quickly discovered that breaking the habit of torturing herself with worry took some discipline. For starters, Marie was often unconscious of the moments that obsessive worrying started to creep into her thought process until she had been swept away by this self-defeating habit.

To break this habit, Marie began by scheduling an hour a day to consciously focus on overdramatizing her situation and worrying like a maniac! This made an unconscious process into a conscious one for her. Once that hour was over, Marie committed to pausing in order to deal with what was right in front of her in the most powerful manner possible for the rest of the day.

Like many clients, Marie also realized that she often rushed around under pressure. Thus, she found it helpful to take a couple of hours a week to discipline herself to move at half of her normal speed. During the hours she set aside to train herself to operate in a more senatorial manner, Marie focused on breathing, staying deliberately conscious of her physical pace, and sharpening her focus on the nuances of what was happening around her in the moment.

It worked. Thanks to her efforts at retraining herself, Marie eventually found that her inner iceberg got smaller.

In short order, Marie found that she was less prone to darting around nervously on the job. She also wasn't as distracted by anxious thoughts in her staff meetings. As these simple changes became normalized, Marie also became mindful that her impulse to hastily "fix things" was often driven more by a Big Ship need for personal validation than by a desire to pursue a workable solution. Practicing the skill of pausing helped Marie to trust herself more and to focus on workable solutions for the greater good.

### 3: Marie Evaluates Her Skills and Resources

Next, Marie assessed her professional situation from a broader perspective. As she did this, Marie realized that, not only had her expectations of herself been distorted, her expectations of others had been skewed as well.

As Marie became less judgmental of herself and her own feelings, she became less defensive. As she became less defensive, she became less prone to isolate.

Gradually, it dawned on her that her colleagues might be helpful resources for dealing with Nancy. Having grasped the importance of listening to herself, Marie started to listen more carefully to her team. She asked them about their experiences and how they dealt with Nancy, and this provided Marie with more options for improving this client relationship.

In addition, as her fear lessened, Marie stopped getting caught up in the frantic busywork that had been draining her personally. This was the point in the Lifeboat Process where Marie discovered something important. She realized that she had developed a self-sabotaging habit of reflexively placating Nancy under pressure.

An anxious approval seeker, Marie slowed down enough to recognize this negative thought pattern, which operated beneath her conscious awareness and was undermining her effectiveness. This had become a lifelong habit of acting sugary sweet on the outside at precisely the moment she was boiling mad on the inside. Upon reflection, Marie decided she had developed this habit to keep herself from exploding!

This had to stop, since it undermined her strengths and behavior under pressure, and it undermined her leadership, since she was inadvertently coming across as a doormat in front of others when Nancy walked all over her in tense meetings.

Eventually, rather than being flummoxed by Nancy's childish

behavior, Marie realized that her experience as a parent had given her the skills necessary to resolve the situation. This was one of Marie's authentic strengths that, until she slowed down enough to put her situation into better perspective, had been hidden in plain sight.

Marie decided to take back her power by adjusting her tone and by remaining calm and pragmatic in the face of Nancy's tirades. By this point, she realized that this nonverbal shift would communicate more powerfully to her team than words alone could.

## 4: Marie Develops a Plan and Takes Action

A quick study, Marie came up with two plans of action: one for dealing with Nancy, and one for managing her team. First, at the next team meeting that Nancy attended, Marie decided to demonstrate to everyone that things were going to change.

Nancy, who had falsely accused members of Marie's team of fudging their expenses, was secretly trying to avoid paying expenses altogether so she could show higher revenue numbers. At the meeting, Nancy opened with a simple one-liner she hoped would embarrass Marie enough to silence her and score a quick win.

Pushing the expense reports across the desk toward Marie, Nancy looked her in the eye and said firmly, "Your team has been padding their billable hours. Deny it, and I'll know you are a liar."

Everyone on Marie's team looked anxious. If a client as important as Nancy was upset, their whole department might get replaced.

Marie paused, which she had learned was a powerful way to start. Then she addressed Nancy in a calm and measured tone, asking, "Why would you think that, Nancy?"

"Because the numbers on these time sheets are wrong! I know they are!" Nancy replied almost shrieking. A seasoned manipulator, Nancy was upping the ante emotionally in order to win.

Marie paused longer this time and responded with the firm and kind tone she used when her son wanted to go to the mall before finishing his homework: "Now Nancy, you and I both know that just isn't true. I respect your passion for detail, but you don't need to use inaccurate or inflammatory words to make your point. We are both better than this, and we will both deal with it professionally."

Marie's statement wasn't placating, and it wasn't a plea. There wasn't an ounce of fear in her tone. Marie's measured statement brought everyone back to the present moment, and to the team's astonishment, the focus of the meeting abruptly shifted to the next business topic.

Next, Marie established a weekly meeting for members of her department to brainstorm about creative ways to deal with difficult clients.

Marie was careful not to single out any client, including Nancy, by name. She didn't want to normalize finger-pointing — she just wanted to open the lines of communication so her team could support one another more effectively under pressure.

A central challenge for the department was Nancy's tendency to be a time vampire on the phone. Marie's staff came up with a strategy that involved passing Nancy's calls off to one another so nobody on the team had to converse with Nancy for more than twenty minutes. That way, Nancy couldn't demoralize anyone for too long or keep the team from getting their work done. Marie was glowing with pride the day she watched one of her staff look up at the clock, press hold and give another team member a "thumbs-up" as he picked up the receiver and said with a welcoming tone, "Nancy, it's so great to hear from you! We all want to make sure you are happy."

Over time, Marie began to view Nancy's dysfunctional behavior as a learning opportunity. As Marie said to me, "If the challenges with Nancy hadn't forced me to look within, I might never have noticed the ways that I had been abandoning my team, my family, and even myself."

With this realization, Marie had truly taken her power back. She wasn't thinking from the Big Ship mindset anymore — she had made the Lifeboat shift.

*Lifeboat Question #6*

# WHO CAN I TRUST IN A CRISIS?

Trust isn't conceptual on a lifeboat. It isn't just a word scrawled on a whiteboard during a focus group. Trust is earned — and it can also be squandered. On a lifeboat or in the workplace, the choice of who we trust and why we trust them can have profound consequences to the ways our lives unfold and to our personal integrity.

For the passengers on Lifeboat #6, their situation was the stuff of nightmares. After the *Titanic* sank, they all realized that they had narrowly escaped death, but they were now trapped in a small craft bobbing somewhere in the dark on the Atlantic Ocean, and all around them they could hear the desperate voices of dying people who were still in the water, screaming in terror and begging to be saved.

Could they save anyone else? Could they save themselves? No one knew, but they were keenly aware that, if they were going to survive, they needed one another. None of them could beat the odds alone.

In this chapter, I look at how the Lifeboat Process can help you identify the type of people you can trust and why — particularly in a crisis — by paying attention to certain behavioral characteristics. You can also use these characteristics to critique and guide your own reactions under pressure, so that you become someone others turn to, rely on, and trust. The Lifeboat lessons in this chapter will enhance your leadership capacity and your effectiveness working with colleagues under pressure.

## The Passengers in Lifeboat #6 Face a Choice

Lifeboat #6 was launched with only twenty-nine people, but it could hold sixty-five. It was half-empty when *Titanic* sank, and as the passengers huddled together in the dark listening to the pleas and prayers of their fellow passengers freezing and dying in the ocean, the urgent question arose: Would they return to where *Titanic* had submerged to save others?

While eyewitness testimony can't pinpoint precisely why the power struggle started between Robert Hichens and Arthur Peuchen, survivors do recall that these two men had a strong disagreement about how Lifeboat #6 should respond to these cries for help.

Hichens was stridently vocal about his concerns that trying to pull people from the water might capsize their vessel. In one of history's prime examples of poor word choice, Hichens made the mistake of referring to these unfortunate victims as "stiffs." To put it mildly, this word resonated poorly with the rest of the group.

During the inquiry that followed the disaster, Hichens later denied using the word *stiffs*, and he attempted to justify his conduct on Lifeboat #6 by claiming that he had been acting on last-minute orders from Captain Smith *not* to return for additional survivors. These claims were disputed by others.

In the lifeboat that night, various people in the group joined in the argument and voiced criticism of Hichens, and he became critical of them. Survivors reported that, in the midst of the debate about whether or not to help people struggling in the water, Hichens abruptly changed the subject by lashing out at Frederick Fleet. "Your oar is not being put in the water at the proper angle!" he barked at Fleet. Upon hearing this, several of the female passengers reportedly taunted Hichens about taking an oar himself!

Most of the women on board had no idea how to handle an oar, and as they huddled together freezing, they hoped the men could figure things out! In response to these taunts, Hichens sulked. The trust between the group and their formal leader was breaking down.

Peuchen, who had also been trying to get Hichens to row, reportedly addressed the female passengers by telling them, "It's no use arguing with this man at all. It's best not to discuss matters with him."

Hichens clearly resented having his authority questioned; he clung to his status as the nominal leader, even though the entire group was in disagreement with him. At some point during this back and forth, Hichens noticed Margaret Brown and how she was quietly organizing the female passengers to start rowing. Hichens didn't like it, and he swore at Brown and tried to physically stop her and the other women from rowing.

At this, Brown had finally had enough. She threatened to throw Hichens overboard if he didn't back down, close his mouth, and keep his pessimism to himself! The other passengers voiced their support of Brown, and Hichens backed off. Afterward, Hichens became even more detached from the others. Once the rest of the group refused to recognize his authority, his ability and desire to lead evaporated.

When Brown found her voice and spoke up, everything changed. Her message embodied the Lifeboat mindset, and everyone recognized this, even Peuchen and Fleet. The force of her emotion sparked everyone (except perhaps Hichens) to make the Lifeboat shift, uniting them all. Her message, felt as much as spoken, encouraged everyone to trust in themselves and to trust one another.

The words we speak often stem from the silent conversations we have in our heads. I've often imagined Margaret Brown, as she listened to Hichens voice his despair, pushing back in her mind by uttering to herself something like, "Not today! I'm going to see my grandson again! These women are going to see their loved ones again! No matter what you tell us, we aren't quitting!"

Feelings are contagious: Fear is contagious, and trust is contagious. Brown's defiance and determination caused a wave of encouragement to spread through the group and envelop them. Brown gave voice to something that was simmering beneath the surface in the hearts and minds of her fellow passengers. Hichens was running on fear and creating conflict, but if they were going to make it, they needed a leader who could unite them.

Further, in spite of the fear engulfing them all, Margaret Brown was doing her best to support the physical and emotional needs of her fellow passengers. Brown was treating everyone as equals and with respect. She didn't criticize the women for their lack of experience with watercraft, nor did she jump into the fray as Hichens and Peuchen argued over what to do and who should be in command. Brown wasn't after status or authority. Brown was simply focused on helping the group survive. As a result, by the time she spoke up, Brown was already taking actions and treating others in a way that embodied the kind of informal leadership that inspires trust in a crisis.

Let's face it, what happened on Lifeboat #6 was a mutiny. Of course, no one on board used this loaded word — not even Hichens — but the passengers took control. Tragically, by this time, the cries of others in the water had faded to silence, and Lifeboat #6 was unable to rescue anyone else.

After their own rescue by the *Carpathia*, most of the Lifeboat #6 survivors had harsh words for Hichens. They had lost respect for him. His refusal to go back to help others earned him the moniker of "the coward." His language offended the rest of the group — from calling drowning people "stiffs" to cursing at Brown, which violated the code of conduct about how to speak to a lady. Worst of all, Hichens hadn't stopped droning on that they were all doomed. This cast a pall over the group and drained their energy until Brown rallied them to keep going.

As Brown's behavior illustrates, to inspire the trust of others, we must demonstrate the ability to trust ourselves. While many things in life can be faked, our ability to trust ourselves when we face the unknown isn't one of them. On a lifeboat where people are bunched together with their lives on the line, or in a workplace when our financial security and reputations hang in the balance, words alone don't count for much. Facial expressions, glances, and the smallest gestures can convey truths that words could never capture. When the stakes are this high, nuances that might have been overlooked on the Big Ship can become glaring signals that guide our choices.

On a lifeboat, there's nowhere to hide — even from yourself.

## Status and Roles Don't Matter on a Lifeboat

Picture the *Titanic* pulling out of the harbor amid cheers and fanfare at the beginning of that fateful trip. The roles and relationships among the people on board were dictated by their status in the crew or their ticket price. If you had a first-class ticket for this voyage, no expense was spared to make sure that you dined on fine china and enjoyed mouthwatering meals. Nobody questioned this; that was the promise of sailing on a Big Ship. People trusted this promise.

Once the *Titanic* sank, the relevance of everyone's Big Ship status sank with it. In a lifeboat, it suddenly didn't matter what your rank was among the crew, how much you paid for your trip, or whether you dined at the captain's table. Everyone needed to work together to survive, and this prioritized other attributes: the courage to face one's fears and not be overwhelmed; the ability to communicate effectively under pressure; and the desire to support and save everyone, not just oneself.

In this new reality, who to trust and why to trust them was in flux.

Everyone agrees that people matter. However, on a Big Ship, this is often an abstract idea that's ignored when it's inconvenient. For people who are living in a bubble of luxury, many things, including relationships, can feel expendable. If someone doesn't give you what you want, you fire them and find someone who will!

On a lifeboat, no one is expendable, and even more important than any single individual's skills, experiences, and strengths is for the group to unify with the common purpose of bringing everyone to safety. Someone's willingness to be present for and support the group is what earns them the trust of others in a crisis. On a lifeboat, there's no status to shield you, no laurels to rest on, and no "game face" left. There's you, an oar, and your attitude. And your attitude, making the Lifeboat shift, may be the thing that saves everyone.

This can certainly be seen when a crisis hits the workplace. Industry leaders, or anyone accustomed to the perks of senior management, may find it difficult at first to make the Lifeboat shift, since this levels the status of everyone. But it's often a relief to rank-and-file employees, and they may especially appreciate senior executives who jump into a lifeboat to save their companies and everyone's livelihoods. When this happens, everyone grabs an oar — and there's no room for excess baggage. From the Lifeboat mindset, an attitude of entitlement weighs someone down like an anchor — so pitch it!

However, even more often, my clients describe company leaders and executives who act more like Robert Hichens under pressure. When a crisis strikes, who will you turn to for help in your company? Can you trust your senior management team? Can you trust human resources to support you?

As an executive coach, I've witnessed the devastating professional consequences that befall people who turn for help to bosses and leaders who prove untrustworthy and who don't act in the best interests of others or the group. When a power struggle erupts out of nowhere, people sometimes march defiantly into a senior manager's office to unload their frustration and ask for assistance, and later they are often bewildered when they find themselves passed over for promotion. When managers complain to HR that unrealistic work demands are harming the emotional and physical health of their staff, they are often stunned when they find themselves eased out of their positions during an unexpected wave of downsizing. Big Ship leaders who don't want to face problems or change course may "solve" those problems by removing the people issuing the warnings or asking for change.

Ultimately, adopting the Lifeboat mindset means recognizing that, no matter what company you work for or your professional status, you will face situations that you can't handle alone. When this happens, you will need the help of people you can trust. Choosing those people wisely may make the difference between failure and survival, but sometimes, you don't know who you can truly rely on until a crisis hits.

The stories of the *Titanic* survivors teach us that the *first* person you have to learn to trust is yourself. In the last chapter, we discussed ways that you can prepare yourself to operate more effectively under pressure. Like Brown, we train ourselves to pause under pressure and connect with a part of ourselves that's rooted in something deeper than logic. What we are connecting with is our felt sense of inner alignment. It's this sense of inner alignment that confirms that our thoughts and feelings are proportionate to the situation at hand. This inner safety check helps us focus our mental and emotional energy so that we can identify the next positive action we can take in the moment, collaborate effectively with others, and pursue solutions that reinforce our authentic values.

This same sense of inner alignment can help you discern who may or may not be trustworthy under pressure. Whether your journey is across the ocean or up the corporate ladder, putting your trust in the right people is vital to achieving your goals.

## Trusting Yourself: Recognize Conditioning and Admit Vulnerability

For many people, the conditioning that limits their ability to connect authentically with others and to trust themselves starts early in life.

Becoming conditioned to operate from the Big Ship mindset often stems from the behavioral norms people have been exposed to in their family systems. Many of us were raised by caregivers who, in an attempt to keep us from harm's way and socialize us to fit into the wider world, did their best to teach us to follow the Big Ship rules.

Do it right, and you get the carrot.

Do it wrong, and you get the stick.

These attitudes can condition us to judge ourselves, others, and the world primarily based on external results, and this normalizes a transactional approach to relationships: We need external validation to feel good about and to trust ourselves, and our status relative to others often guides our behavior and treatment of people, rather than compassion and ethics. This Big Ship mindset encourages people to cultivate, defend, and hide behind their image or official role. Like Hichens, people will sometimes break their bonds with others and isolate themselves to protect this image when it's threatened. You can't count on Big Ship thinkers under pressure if their first concern is for themselves and how they're seen.

That's why, in order to continue to improve your ability to trust yourself, it's important to consider the ways you've been conditioned to view relationships. To do this, you need to examine how you react when you feel vulnerable. No one likes to feel vulnerable, and we avoid it if at all possible. But that's part of what defines a crisis: We are threatened and need help. When that happens to you, do you tend to panic, freeze, deny the crisis, insist you can handle it alone, or take charge to look strong? If so, can you learn to recognize that tendency and instead make the Lifeboat shift? Can you admit to being afraid and vulnerable, and then work with others to make wise decisions under pressure to solve common problems? Remember, in a crisis, what's most important isn't your skills and training in a particular job. It's your attitude. This is what allows us, when we face an unwelcome surprise, to put aside our roles and do what needs to be done, while learning to trust others based on their attitudes, not their status.

To trust yourself in a crisis, you have to be able to squarely face the areas where you feel most vulnerable — these are the difficult emotions that make up your inner iceberg. If you can't admit to feeling vulnerable, then under pressure, your primary concern will be denying or hiding your difficult emotions and vulnerability, not solving the problem.

For example, let's consider the so-called alpha personality type. An alpha personality is someone who tends to assume a dominant role in social or professional situations, and they tend to be very competitive. They play to win, and while they may help others, they always want to be the one on top. Alphas hate vulnerability. They hate it in themselves — and they hate it in others.

As Margaret Brown demonstrates, the Lifeboat shift means dropping concerns over status and personal vulnerability and treating everyone as important, as someone who can help and who deserves help. If we act this way all the time, we help inspire the trust of others all the time — not just in a crisis. Further, we will gain self-confidence, since we will know both how to inspire trust and how to recognize a trustworthy person, which may one day be vital to our survival. Remember, not everyone makes the Lifeboat shift — even when they are literally in a lifeboat!

Let's start by examining the "Big Ship relationship characteristics" described below.

## Big Ship Relationship Characteristics

The *Titanic* story shows us that learning who to trust in a crisis is a survival skill. Most of us are unlikely to ever be on a ship that hits an actual iceberg, but we *are* likely to hit an unexpected professional setback that can sink our careers.

With this in mind, let's consider four Big Ship relationship characteristics. These are four behavioral "warning signs" that indicate people who are so steeped in Big Ship thinking that we should proceed with caution. Learn to spot these tendencies and use them to help guide your decisions about who to trust. That said, observing this type of behavior in someone doesn't necessarily mean that they can't be trusted in a crisis; after all, Captain Smith made the Lifeboat shift, even if Robert Hichens did not. Some people rise to the occasion under pressure and become more genuine than we would expect!

Here are the four behaviors that epitomize Big Ship relationship characteristics:

1. **Make a dazzling first impression:** Some people arrive trying to impress others any way they can, wearing status symbols, emphasizing their awards and accomplisments, and name-dropping.

2. **Be dramatic:** Some people use their emotional energy to dominate others, whether sweeping people off their feet with passion or using anger to tip people off-balance or freeze them in their tracks.

3. **Monopolize the conversation:** Some people keep the spotlight on themselves, always have to have the last word, or will say whatever is necessary to get their own way.

4. **Associate primarily with others who enhance one's image:** Some people only invest their time and energy in relationships that boost their own status. This transactional attitude means they rarely pay attention to or care about anyone they can't get something from.

These Big Ship relationship characteristics are natural extensions of the Big Ship rules (pages 41–43): They focus on impression management. The Big Ship mindset prioritizes having the biggest network, getting the most attention, and anything that adds to one's external status. This is in part because, on a Big Ship, people often don't get rewarded for being authentic — they get rewarded for playing their role. This is why people sometimes feel "better than" or "less than" others depending upon their place in the Big Ship hierarchy.

Another way to determine who to trust in a crisis is paying attention to how you feel about yourself after you have been in someone's presence. Does being around someone leave you feeling validated and inspired or do you feel deflated or anxious? Pay attention to your intuition in addition to observing particular behaviors. Sometimes, we can't quite define why we feel certain ways, but that doesn't mean those feelings are inaccurate or wrong. In such a case, what can clarify your reaction is getting feedback from someone you trust who is outside of the situation (see "Lifeboat Feedback: Identifying an Inner Iceberg," pages 142–47).

That said, don't passively accept other people's opinions about who does or does not merit your trust. This is a form of giving away your power, and it can be a career killer. Whether you are trying to identify the right people to build a high-performing team, negotiating a strategic alliance, or working to build a motivational culture across your organization, use observation, intuition, and trusted feedback to make your own decisions. Then, in a crisis, pay attention to what people do and whether being under pressure causes them to change — in either helpful or negative ways.

## LIFEBOAT CASE STUDY, PART 1
### Janet Admits Her Vulnerability

Janet, a marketing executive for a successful hedge fund, started working with me when her company hired a new CEO who initiated a firm-wide restructuring effort. Janet had reached out for coaching because her experience with the head of marketing, Susan, was undermining her self-confidence so severely that she was concerned about her ability to trust herself on the job.

"Some days, I can barely get out of bed in the morning," Janet confessed during our initial meeting. "My boss, Susan, always seems to offer me advice in a way that leaves me feeling anxious about how I'm being perceived by others."

This was a strong start for Janet. By reaching out for feedback, Janet was being honest with herself about her genuine feelings on the job. One of the challenges of making the Lifeboat shift is that admitting genuine vulnerability can be risky in an organization that rewards people based on the image they project.

"Can you give me an example of this?" I asked her.

"We were sharing a car on the way back from the airport after a presentation to the new senior management team last week," Janet told me. "My part of the presentation was a discussion of how we could leverage what we were doing with our existing clients to help support the efforts of the sales division and, out of nowhere, Susan got really upset." Janet's breath grew shallow and she spoke rapidly as she shared this part of the story.

"What do you mean by upset?" I asked.

"Susan actually started crying because she was so angry with me," Janet replied. "I thought my comments were helpful, and the head of sales actually came over to us after my comments, shook my hand, and congratulated Susan for having such great talent on her team! Susan was beaming and joining in the praise while he was complimenting me. However, once we were alone in the car together, Susan started ripping my presentation to shreds. She brought up all these little ways that I hadn't come across as senior enough to be the kind of reflection on our department she had hoped for, and then she started insinuating that I was trying to play up to the sales guys at her expense."

"How did you respond?" I asked.

"I didn't," Janet admitted, looking down sadly at her hands. "I just prayed that we'd get back quickly and that she'd forget the whole thing the next day. The really crazy part of this is that the next day, Susan came in smiling brightly as if nothing had happened. I've been tirelessly supportive of her and helped her get promoted to head our department. However, these days, I honestly don't know where I stand with her. It's very distressing."

Like many people working for a boss who fosters self-doubt among subordinates, Janet was feeling isolated and losing confidence. By having a frank and emotionally honest discussion about this, Janet was taking a first step toward breaking the isolation that was amplifying her insecurity. Summoning the courage to be honest when we feel vulnerable builds the personal confidence necessary to take constructive action. Janet needed to take this step before she could take her power back on the job. The next step was to examine her feelings as objectively as possible, which meant getting feedback from a trusted observer.

## Lifeboat Feedback: Identifying an Inner Iceberg

The feedback Janet got from her boss was undermining her ability to trust herself. This had triggered an inner iceberg of fear, panic, and confusion. She felt herself sinking, and she knew she needed to clarify what she was feeling and what had gone wrong before she could figure out how to save herself.

Although Janet had taken the initial step of admitting her vulnerability and the need for help, she was still being tossed around by waves of emotion. She was being dragged down by feelings of self-doubt, anger, resentment, and even shame. This inner vortex of self-doubt was draining her energy and undermining her ability to see clearly and take constructive action.

When we encounter an inner iceberg, we can sometimes understand it and identify how it arose on our own, but frequently, we need the perspective of someone we trust to clarify and verify our reactions and the situation. Recognizing an inner iceberg requires emotional honesty, and getting Lifeboat feedback from a trusted observer practices the skill of emotional honesty with others.

In fact, getting Lifeboat feedback helps us master the skills we need in order to communicate with ourselves and others more effectively. It helps us overcome any Big Ship conditioning and the urge to intellectualize and avoid our feelings. Getting the support and feedback of someone you trust is part of the process of learning how to trust yourself. It's even integral to the Lifeboat shift, since by asking for feedback, you take concrete action to avoid isolation. You don't need to speak to a wide circle of people. All you need is one individual whose presence makes you feel safe enough to be emotionally honest.

Pick someone you trust and respect who feels comfortable being emotionally honest themselves and who embodies the Lifeboat mindset (whether they think in those terms or not). Ideally, you want the other person to tell you what they really think, not what they think you want to hear or only what makes you "look good." You want someone to provide their genuine impression of the problem and whether or not you are being true to yourself.

If possible, it's helpful to have this conversation with someone who isn't directly involved in the situation. If the person works at your organization, make sure they don't work in your same department. Candor is enhanced when the person you are talking with doesn't have a vested interest in the outcome.

This feedback is intended to help you clarify the interplay of thoughts and feelings that constitute your inner iceberg, which is essential for making wise decisions about the effective actions you can take. It's also designed to help you get underneath the words you tend to use to describe things to yourself and others. An objective observer can help you sort through the nonverbal cues you are displaying while you talk. This can enhance your awareness of the underlying meaning that a particular situation may have for you and help you develop an action plan that's proportionate, practical, and effective.

There are basically two parts to the process: First, you describe the difficult person and situation as clearly and objectively as possible. Then, you ask the other person a series of questions that invite them to evaluate your clarity and honesty and ask for feedback about your understanding of the situation. The point isn't to invite judgments or engage in finger-pointing. You don't address who is right or who is wrong. The goal is to assess and confirm your self-honesty and awareness of this situation. When you're unsure whether you can trust yourself under pressure, one way to decide is to check in with someone you trust and ask them!

## Part 1: Tell Your Story

The first part is simple. You talk and the other person listens.

Describe the professional relationship that you find particularly challenging. Be as specific as possible to give a clear picture of the particular aspects of the situation that are triggering you. You may want to write these down beforehand to make sure you include everything that is important.

To the best of your ability, be candid about your emotional reactions to the situation and this challenging individual. Don't sugarcoat it — get real.

While you speak, the listener has two important jobs. The first is to ask clarifying questions if they are unclear about anything or if they feel you might be oversimplifying "messy" details or speaking in generalities to "look good." Even when we mean to be candid and honest, we might still try to avoid feelings of vulnerability, or Big Ship conditioning might lead us to minimize or deny issues that undermine our self-image. Remember, the Lifeboat mindset is about honestly assessing what is happening in the present moment.

The listener's other job is to confirm their understanding by periodically repeating back what they hear. They should weigh in occasionally to repeat the essence of what you are saying to make sure you both share a common understanding. This also reassures you that you are being heard correctly.

This repetition might seem tedious, and it may require patience. Remember, the Big Ship mindset is always in a hurry! However, repetition is an integral part of releasing frozen feelings. When people tap into buried feelings, which may have accumulated over a long time, they aren't always expressed succinctly. As you describe the situation and your reaction, take all the time you need to express yourself fully, and encourage the other person to keep asking for more details and repeating their understandings until you both feel satisfied.

Finally, it's vital that the listener resist the temptation to offer advice, reframe the situation, or distract you from an authentic account of your experience. To begin, focus only on telling your story as honestly and completely as possible.

### Part 2: Ask Questions and Get Feedback

Once you've finished describing the situation, ask your partner a series of five questions that are intended to help you assess your honesty and your perspective on the situation. Afterward, based on this feedback, you can consider the most effective course of action going forward.

Here are the five questions to ask:

1.  Do you think I sound emotionally honest, or are there any feelings I may be burying or can't admit?

2. What do you think my body language and tone are conveying?

3. Do you think I'm being clear with myself about my motives? If not, what am I missing?

4. Do you think my assessment of the difficult person is objective and fair? If not, what am I missing?

5. Do you think anyone else besides me is being affected by this situation? If so, who and how?

You can ask the questions one at a time or all at once, but then simply listen to the feedback you receive without interrupting. If you hear things you don't understand, ask the person to clarify. However, if you hear things that make you emotionally uncomfortable, keep listening while gently observing what's going on: in your body and with your feelings and thoughts. You may want to jot down some notes about your inner reactions and the comments that are triggering them. This will help you remember the sensations you are experiencing more clearly — and it can ease any urge you may have to interrupt the person.

One of the powerful aspects of this exercise is how the conversations we have with others inform the conversations we are always having with ourselves. Since all communication is both verbal and nonverbal, pay attention to your body. The pace of your breathing and any tension you experience may convey vital information that leads to a fuller understanding of what's playing out in your inner world.

After completing the feedback conversation with your partner, write down any themes that emerged from this discussion and strategize what types of effective action you can take. Consider who you can trust in the situation to help you based on how or whether they seem to embody the Big Ship relationship characteristics or the

Lifeboat values I describe in the next chapter (pages 156–59), where I discuss this step of evaluation and taking effective action.

However, first, to illustrate how this Lifeboat feedback exercise can unfold, let's continue Janet's story. Once Janet realized she needed help to confirm her feelings and trust herself, she reached out to her friend Angela. Janet and Angela had worked together on a couple of committees for a women's networking organization, so Angela was familiar with Janet's work style. The feedback Janet got helped clarify the challenges she was facing and strengthened her commitment to make positive changes to solve the unexpected crisis with her job.

## LIFEBOAT CASE STUDY, PART 2
### Janet Asks for Help

"I've always respected women who support other women," Janet told me. "Angela is a wise woman with a great sense of humor. She always makes sure we address timely topics at our business events. While Angela is a straight shooter, she has a positive way of looking at the challenges we both face that helps me put things into a more hopeful perspective."

Janet and Angela cleared a date with both of their families so they could have this discussion over dinner at an Italian restaurant. Janet said, "I wanted to pick a time and place for this Lifeboat exercise with the same care I would devote to planning a meeting with an important client or a prospective employer. I realized that this dinner with Angela was going to be positive for my professional development, and it could potentially lead to insights we could both use to help others. I wanted us to both enjoy every moment of it."

Even though Angela was a trusted friend, Janet was a little anxious to share her experience so candidly. This is natural. When we have been operating from the Big Ship mindset, we've been living in a competitive world where emotional vulnerability can be used against us. However, Janet courageously explained her situation to Angela, along with the confrontation with Susan in the car leaving the airport, and then listened as Angela provided feedback to the five questions.

## 1. "Do you think I sound emotionally honest?"

"Let me start by letting you know how much credit I give you after hearing this," Angela began thoughtfully. "I've known you for over four years, and I've never heard you complain about your boss once. I had no idea you were working for a woman who struggled with such passionate displays of insecurity in private. I really feel for you. I also feel like I understand your commitment to helping other women at a much deeper level now. You validate them constantly because you know what it feels like to work like a dog and not get validated yourself."

Janet told me later that Angela's opening was so shockingly positive that it brought tears to her eyes. Positive feedback often takes people who have buried their feelings off guard. However, like many people conditioned by the Big Ship mindset, Janet didn't fully trust compliments. While she was blotting her tears with a napkin, she was also secretly wondering if she would get any original insights that could help her relate to Susan in a more powerful manner.

"That said," Angela continued, "you are letting Susan manipulate you. Since you are a smart woman, at some level you realize this. If somebody treated me like this, I'd be angry. However, I suspect that the reason you don't want to get out of bed some days isn't just because you are angry at Susan — I suspect you might also be angry with yourself."

## 2. "What do you think my body language and tone are conveying?"

"I'm not sure if you realized how often you cast your eyes downward, and your posture looked subservient and apologetic as you were telling me about this," Angela continued. "If you are trying to make Susan feel comfortable by placating her, this may be having the opposite effect. If Susan is looking for someone she can dominate, your tone and body language may be giving her an open invitation."

## 3. "Do you think I'm being clear with myself about my motives?"

Angela said, "There's no doubt about the fact that everyone wants to do a good job at your firm, since it is undergoing a senior management change. The good news is that you were noticed in a public and positive way by the head of your sales division at the presentation. That's great stuff.

"Where your motives sound murky, however, stems from the part of the situation where you get bogged down in whether or not Susan is validating you. Susan's emotional outburst in the car with you was extremely unprofessional — and calculating. If she can get you to personalize her behavior, she can manipulate you more easily."

Angela warned Janet, "In short, if one of your motives is to get Susan to validate you, you may need a reality check. Susan doesn't sound like a safe person for you to turn to for an accurate reflection of your value."

## 4. "Do you think my assessment of the difficult person is objective and fair?"

"Now, perhaps I'm biased here, but the main person you don't seem to be fair to in this situation is yourself," Angela continued. "This goes back to what may be your murky motives in this situation. It's like you are assuming that if you put your nose to the grindstone long enough, Susan is going to have a change of heart and validate you the way you try to validate the women we support through our networking organization.

"One of the things I respect about you is that you work hard to get ahead, and you reward others who operate the same way. However, we both know that not everyone who climbs the corporate ladder plays fair. Some people get ahead by looking for areas where other people are vulnerable and walking over their backs to advance. Whether she realizes it or not, that sounds like what Susan is doing.

"Now, in fairness to Susan, I don't know her and I'm only hearing your side of the story," Angela said thoughtfully. "Senior management changes are always scary, and everyone wants to be noticed. However, if Susan is a person who tantrums whenever she's not in the center of the spotlight, that's not your problem and it's not your work. You've got a job description, and I doubt it contains anything about feeling guilty when Susan can't share credit with others. You need to focus on your work — Susan's emotional baggage is her work."

### 5. "Do you think anyone else besides me is being affected by this situation?"

"If this dynamic continues, you won't be the only one who notices," Angela said with confidence. "Whenever a new management team comes on board, they carefully watch the relational dynamics that play out.

"Even if you are the only person Susan erupts with emotionally, the other members of your department who witness this will be affected. They will start keeping their heads down, hiding in their offices, and doing anything they can to avoid being the next target.

The hidden costs to any organization of a department that's sinking into a fear-based culture eventually hit the bottom line. While talent retention is always important, your most expensive problems mount when people start bringing their bodies to work but they're too anxious to fully focus on their jobs.

"If you stay focused on how your role benefits the organization and try to set some emotional boundaries so Susan doesn't play with your head, things may evolve in a way that's more positive than you might expect," Angela told Janet reassuringly.

"What might happen?" Janet asked her, longing for something to focus on besides trying to please Susan.

"Well, for starters, you might end up getting Susan's job or being moved into a management position in another division," Angela mused. "After all, if your firm brought in an emotional terrorist to wipe out your division, this person would be hard pressed to discourage people as thoroughly as Susan seems to be discouraging you. Susan's management style is costly in many ways, and new management teams tend to focus on getting costs under control."

*Lifeboat Question #7*

# HOW DO WE SURVIVE TOGETHER?

When planning a trip on the open seas, my husband, Charles, spends a great deal of time making sure that our boat's equipment and rigging is in top shape. He is an experienced sailor, and we love to take day trips out into the ocean where we can no longer see land. Having nothing visible but water on all sides seems to restore our perspective and wash away our stress.

Of course, one of the assumptions that makes this type of day peaceful is knowing we will be able to get back.

Charles is vigilant about his navigational equipment and always reminds our family that "if you are two degrees off course and you can still see land, it's no big deal. But miles out on the open seas, if you go two degrees astray, it takes time and effort to get back on course. That can be a problem."

Through the choppy waters of raising teenagers and supporting elderly parents, Charles has always turned to me and said, "Tell me when you feel that I'm two degrees off course." As a hardworking couple, this concept has helped us avoid icebergs, external and internal, and find our way back to peaceful shores.

As I discuss in the previous chapter, in the workplace, running into "difficult people" is a common problem that can sink us or pull us off course. As Janet experienced, if you work with people who make you feel exploited or unappreciated, you risk losing the self-confidence you need to succeed. Of course, what constitutes a "difficult person" or a challenging situation is subjective. It differs for everyone. However, regardless of the specifics, we all encounter adversity, and when that happens, it can trigger our inner iceberg. Then, once we circumnavigate that — perhaps using the feedback of trusted friends and advisors who can tell us if we're two degrees off course — we still need to solve the original problem!

To do that, we often need the help and cooperation of others. We may need the assistance and aid of coworkers and employees who are also affected by the problem, since metaphorically speaking, we can't row the lifeboat alone. What actions we need to take — what it means to "row the lifeboat" — also varies and depends on the circumstances. Remember, the Big Ship attitude is to save yourself, even at the expense of others. In contrast, the Lifeboat attitude is to try to save everyone by working together.

## Lifeboat #6: Mutual Support and Cooperation Save the Day

Margaret Brown wasn't a trained seafarer. Nonetheless, her compassion for the individual struggles of everyone in Lifeboat #6 and the tone she fostered within the group inspired them to follow her guidance in the middle of the ocean when their lives were on the line. Brown's actions on that lifeboat displayed a passionate, positive focus for everyone's survival that inspired her fellow passengers to choose her as their informal leader.

Margaret Brown wasn't trying to advance in the pecking order. Brown was trying to stay focused on what she, and everyone else, could do in the present to survive their deadly predicament. Mindful of the fragile mood and fears of her fellow passengers, she realized that keeping them focused and calm was critical. Rather than setting a tone where people felt pitted against one another to be "good enough," she inspired the group to look out for ways to support one another so that they all survived together.

The more Brown was able to keep the group focused on supporting one another, the stronger they got. A critical mass of passengers on that lifeboat started to realize how vital it was for them to stay mindful of one another's attitudes and well-being. They couldn't afford to tyrannize or demoralize anyone — they needed everyone's physical and emotional stamina to survive.

As the minutes and hours passed, the more everyone became attuned to everyone else's verbal and nonverbal cues. This alignment within the group generated a tone of positive reinforcement everyone could tap into as a source of collective strength. They weren't just trying to collaborate conceptually; they genuinely felt unified.

By quelling the impatience, drama, and ego that the Big Ship mindset can foster, Brown modeled a leadership style that helped Arthur Peuchen make the Lifeboat shift and give her his unqualified support. After Robert Hichens sat back down and ceded his authority to others, Brown and Peuchen worked together as a team. They both recognized that they had complementary strengths. They weren't jockeying for position. They joined forces and stayed focused on the main problem: living long enough to be rescued by another ship.

From a pragmatic perspective, it's clear that the maritime experience of Peuchen and Frederick Fleet were also crucial to the group's survival. Margaret Brown knew her strengths and her limits, and she knew everyone needed the expertise of these two trained sailors. As the informal leader, Brown also instinctively realized she didn't need to have all the answers. By exhibiting a calm leadership style, she helped set a tone that made it possible for these two seaman to lend their experience to the group most effectively. This moment in the *Titanic* story showcases an important lesson for formal and informal leaders alike: Nobody knows everything. Success stems from creating an environment that makes it possible for other people's strengths to flourish. Brown focused on establishing the group's interpersonal rapport. She worked to convince everyone to do the little things that might ensure everyone's survival.

Many things in life simply can't be accomplished alone. Margaret Brown couldn't have made it alone, either. It wasn't enough that she didn't panic when she found herself adrift at sea in a lifeboat; she needed the help of her fellow passengers — and they needed her.

Similarly, personally making the Lifeboat shift and circumnavigating your inner iceberg is not enough. You need other people to help solve the problem, which requires fostering a sense of togetherness, cooperation, and joint effort. Doing that means embodying what I call "Lifeboat values," which are in many ways the opposite of the Big Ship relationship characteristics I describe in the previous chapter.

## Lifeboat Values

Lifeboat values embody a personal commitment to being genuine, to aligning our values with our actions, and to supporting others in a spirit of shared humanity — particularly under pressure. It's the attitude that, whatever happens, we are all in this together. You can't go it alone, and people aren't expendable. You can't hide behind the story you'd like to tell yourself to justify abandoning others or throwing someone overboard. To work together as a group, you have to face the truth of what's unfolding for everyone in the moment.

Embodying Lifeboat values fosters authentic connections with others. Over time, this approach to interacting with others helps every individual in a group clarify his or her values and act in accordance with them. Aligning our actions with our values promotes courage. This type of courage is infectious. It facilitates powerful alliances because it encourages people to combine their strengths in the service of a goal that is genuinely meaningful for everyone — individually and collectively.

Of course, this is the opposite of the Big Ship mindset, which we have explored throughout. The Big Ship rules emphasize playing our part, staying busy, and moving fast. As we have noted, this approach can cause us to dismiss warnings, ignore others, and crash into problems. As a result, the Big Ship mindset can leave us feeling like we are all alone together.

In contrast, Lifeboat values define success from the inside out. You tap into your innate strengths to align your thoughts and feelings with your actions in the present moment — not just to save yourself, but to save the group.

Lifeboat values provide a powerful contrast to the emphasis on keeping up appearances that is stressed by the Big Ship mindset. I summarize them in four ways:

1. **Be genuine and align words with actions**: Rather than try to dazzle others with our credentials, expertise, accomplishments, or style, we attempt to establish a meaningful connection with others. Part of being genuine is ensuring that our words and actions are aligned, which inspires trust and confidence.

2. **Practice empathy**: Rather than try to influence others through dramatic displays of emotion, we focus on understanding what other people may be feeling. We pay attention

both to what people say and to nuances of body language or tone that convey a deeper meaning or unspoken truths. We know that by genuinely noticing, validating, and appreciating others, this encourages others to do the same.

3. **Listen patiently:** Rather than dominating or monopolizing conversations with our own thoughts and opinions, we ask others to share what they think and feel. This is pragmatic, since we need to know what others think in order to build consensus and strategize effective actions. Everyone in a group wants to contribute in meaningful ways to its success. To foster the conditions that make this possible for any group, everyone must be encouraged to look for the value their peers bring rather than compete with their colleagues under pressure.

4. **Don't strive to "look good"; strive to "be good":** Rather than working with or helping only those people who can support our personal agenda, or only doing jobs that enhance our image, we do whatever is necessary to support the group. Rather than grabbing short-term credit, we focus on adding long-term value. Whenever we solve a problem, we also model an approach to problem solving that embraces the relational lesson the group is facing in order to work together more effectively. This approach transforms every crisis into an opportunity to strengthen the group and their commitment to one another.

Operating according to Lifeboat values means realizing that collaboration and teamwork aren't just words. They are values that can elude us during difficult times. That's why we do the inner work necessary to be prepared to act in accord with these values when we need them most — under pressure.

In the Lifeboat mindset, we expect problems and conflict to arise. These conflicts are embraced as learning opportunities. We know obstacles may force us to slow down or change course. We know that when things don't go right, awkward feelings, painful memories, and fears are likely to emerge. But by circumnavigating these inner icebergs individually and collectively, we continue to build skills that enhance our ability to collaborate with others effectively.

In a crisis, not only do we seek to embody Lifeboat values, but they can become a lens for evaluating others and deciding who to work with, who to trust, and whether or not the ship we are on is headed in the right direction. As we clarify the questions we ask ourselves under pressure, we become better at charting our own course professionally. Are people working at this company only for the paycheck, or are they also focused on developing a professional community in which every individual is appreciated? Is collaboration rewarded? Is the group united in the service of a common purpose?

When we recognize people who are focused on what's unfolding in the present and taking the next right action — as opposed to getting into power struggles over who has the right to call the shots — those are people we want to partner with in an unexpected crisis.

## LIFEBOAT CASE STUDY, PART 3
### Janet Takes Action

Like many of us, Janet was trained to turn to her boss to get a gauge of whether or not she was performing effectively on the job. In a perfect world, this would have involved Susan validating Janet for the contributions she was making that supported the department's efforts and mentoring Janet in areas where she needed additional support.

That wasn't happening, and let's face it: It's never a perfect world. Susan's negative attitude and unhelpful behavior were undermining Janet's self-esteem and, as Angela pointed out, likely impacting everyone else in the group. Thus, Janet faced two problems: First, as an individual, Janet needed to put Susan's reactions into perspective, rebuild her self-confidence, and think for herself. Second, as a leader, Janet also had to do what she could to support her team and foster positive results.

Margaret Brown had a similar dilemma. As Robert Hichens, the designated leader of Lifeboat #6, broke down, his attitude and behavior endangered everyone. As an individual, Brown had to cope with Hichens, but Brown also needed the group to work together so they could all survive. What's more, Brown needed to tackle both of these challenges without losing precious time and energy by getting into a power struggle with anyone!

After getting Lifeboat feedback from Angela, Janet decided to do some soul searching about what she looked for in leaders that inspired her. What resonated with her most were leaders who found a strategic balance between confidence and humility. This prompted Janet to draw on the principles she used while mentoring young women in the networking organization she and Angela were involved with. The mentoring work they did wasn't about "looking good" or enhancing their status; it was all about interacting with young women from their industry who needed support in the early years of their careers to advance.

With these principles in mind, Janet used the Lifeboat Process to put her reactions to Susan's outbursts into perspective. Getting around this inner iceberg helped her stop obsessing about her boss. In addition, Janet also began looking for ways to embody the type of leadership she admired and which her department sorely lacked. She focused on being positive and encouraging productive efforts.

By clarifying what she could do to support her department, Janet found that she became much more timely and observant when it came to validating her colleagues and pointing out their strengths.

This approach echoed the way that Margaret Brown established rapport with her fellow passengers on Lifeboat #6. Brown, as we know, added value to the group's effort not based on a personal agenda but from a commitment to noticing and supporting everyone's efforts as they coped with survival at sea.

This is how informal leaders are born. Janet was already the second-most senior member of the group after Susan, but as time passed, Janet gradually started to be recognized by others as the department's informal leader.

Janet's experience illustrates how operating according to Lifeboat values not only helps us survive — it can help us thrive. Here is what happened:

## Be Authentic and Aligned, and Avoid Superficial Impression Management

As events unfolded, Janet practiced pausing as much as possible. Pausing was essential for Janet to consistently act in alignment with her values. Without pausing, Janet realized she would risk slipping back into self-defeating negative reactions to Susan's behavior.

For instance, Janet used to get particularly distracted by Susan's behavior whenever the firm made a new hire at the senior executive level. This was because Susan always lobbied to be one of the first people at the firm to help this individual onboard. Because Susan was such a harsh manager when it came to dealing with her own team, watching how impressed senior management appeared to be with the way Susan ingratiated herself with new hires drove Janet and members of her team nuts.

Here's why.

Getting their department ready for one of Susan's impromptu walkabouts with a new hire, or anyone from the executive floor, felt like cleaning the house for the in-laws before a holiday party.

Susan insisted that everyone's desks be as clear as possible, and personal photos were to be kept to a minimum! She would stalk the halls anxiously prior to one of her "relaxed" strolls with a colleague to glare at anyone whose workspace appeared cluttered.

Once Janet understood how important impression management is to people operating from the Big Ship mindset, Janet stopped obsessing about Susan's anxious behavior before these senior executive visits. The less emotionally triggered she was, the more Janet could focus on being constructive in these moments.

While she made sure to keep her desk clean, Janet also made sure to follow up with everyone who visited their department. She got their contact information and sent them a note to let them know she had enjoyed meeting them and would be happy to reconnect if they had questions in the future.

What was the biggest payoff to this little action? It started to rebuild Janet's confidence in herself! Janet shifted from focusing on Susan's assessment of her value and prioritized how *she* felt about her job performance. This foundational shift helped Janet reclaim her personal power from the inside out. This also helped her respond to Susan's requests without feeling like she was sacrificing her sense of self in the process.

That was a key lesson: By believing in and acting from her authentic self, Janet became more effective.

## Practice Empathy, and Avoid Emotional Volatility and Manipulation

Janet noted that the rest of the staff in their group consistently referred to Susan as a "drama queen." This wasn't a compliment.

Susan had earned this moniker by getting so lost in her own story and carried away by her feelings that she didn't notice when the rest of her team wasn't on the same page with her. One team member once turned to Janet and said, "It's actually easier to get things done without her. When Susan is here, she's too distracted to listen, anyway. I feel completely erased in her presence."

Susan tended to get most volatile in staff meetings when things didn't go according to plan. Susan would summon an emotional intensity that made everyone's blood run cold as she pointed the finger of blame at others, while refusing to accept any personal responsibility.

Janet was so scared of being a target that she rarely spoke up in group meetings when Susan was present.

As Janet found herself continually suppressing her powerful feelings and anger over Susan's behavior, she became more exhausted. She also wanted to fight back! When Susan scapegoated others to avoid taking responsibility, Janet wanted to put Susan in her place! This is natural. But in a lifeboat, power struggles and fights over leadership often don't help. They can divide the group and distract everyone from taking effective, positive action. Remember, Margaret Brown did not seek a confrontation with Robert Hichens; he confronted her, which forced the group to make a decision.

There are times when confrontation is both necessary and constructive. However, when we are operating from Lifeboat values, we pause to assess our intention and the situation before we go there. Are we hitting an inner iceberg? Will speaking up support the group? Is this the best timing? Most important, will the person we are tempted to confront be able to actually listen in this moment?

On Lifeboat #6, Hichens was clearly having an emotional breakdown and couldn't listen effectively to anyone. Hence, Brown focused on where she could add value.

In Janet's case, she knew that directly confronting Susan wouldn't convince her to change (just like Brown didn't try to convince Hichens to change). Plus, the conflict would further erode department morale, and undermining Susan's leadership might force the company to choose between them (and maybe get rid of Janet). Instead, Janet chose to remain calm and centered during these outbursts. One thing that helped was realizing that dramatic, manipulative displays of emotion reflect the Big Ship mindset. Janet didn't need to take them personally, and it wasn't necessarily her responsibility to try to contain Susan when she exploded. Like being in a lifeboat in rough seas, there wasn't much point in shouting at the waves.

The best thing to do was to ride out the turbulence without emotionally capsizing, and Janet found this became easier and easier. Keeping Susan's behavior in perspective, Janet stopped wasting energy beating herself up and suppressing negative reactions. Over time, this growing sense of inner calm not only helped restore her self-esteem, it freed up energy to focus on a more positive approach to professional challenges.

## Listen Patiently, and Avoid Monopolizing Conversations

In any meeting where a member of senior management or one of their staff was in attendance, Susan did her best to be the constant center of attention. Susan's display of this particular Big Ship relational characteristic was an especially powerful emotional trigger for Janet!

In meetings, Janet found herself hitting a huge inner iceberg on this one. Janet's attention would stray from the business matter at hand as she found herself obsessing over the myriad ways Susan managed to control the room through her behavior and to bring attention back to herself. Instead of focusing on work, Janet focused on how Susan folded her arms, squirmed in her chair, and even sighed audibly when she wasn't the center of attention. This made Janet furious, and as her inner iceberg grew from suppressing so much anger, she floundered and felt herself sinking.

This reaction was becoming self-destructive personally as well as professionally. Janet would eat compulsively to soothe herself at night while replaying negative moments from her workday, sometimes writing down all the things Susan did that made her resentful.

Fortunately, as Janet worked with the Lifeboat Process, she got better at anticipating her triggers and managing her inner iceberg. She also realized that Susan was providing important leadership lessons about what *not* to do.

However, after getting feedback from Angela, Janet realized she needed a sounding board on a regular basis, so she could continue processing her feelings. She and Angela agreed to continue meeting for dinner and helping each other make the Lifeboat shift. They frequently reminded each other to pause and remember two acronyms I use with clients grappling with this stage of the Lifeboat Process. These are WAIT and HAIL. WAIT stands for "Why am I talking?" HAIL stands for "How am I listening?"

Using these acronyms helped Janet resist the impulse to give her power away by speaking out impulsively in a no-win situation with her boss, who was unwilling to listen. They also reminded Janet to listen more thoughtfully to others and embody the kind of leadership she admired. Janet began to pay more attention to what the rest of the staff was saying in meetings. She noticed the nonverbal body language of the others in the room — to understand what they *weren't* saying or if they seemed upset — and followed up later with members of her team who looked like they needed her support.

Over time, an interesting shift happened. The same office grapevine that branded Susan a "drama queen" was referring to Janet as one of the best listeners in the firm. Among themselves, the group was making clear who they trusted.

## Be Genuine, and Avoid Striving for Status

Typical of the Big Ship mindset, Susan was transactional in her approach to relationships. She would seduce people who could enhance her image and mentally erase people she couldn't use to advance her agenda.

Susan thought nothing of taking on additional work from members of senior management, or from peers in other departments who were seen as rising stars, if this could enhance her popularity. Of course, this meant overloading her own staff, but she didn't give their workload a second thought.

Janet began noticing a troubling dynamic brewing among her colleagues. The more demoralized and exhausted the team became, the more the group's shared resentment toward Susan led them to mimic Susan's petty behavior in subtle ways.

That's when Janet made a powerful realization. She noticed that relational connections that draw energy from resentments toward a third party are never genuine. The tribal bonding taking place as people blew off steam behind Susan's back had a "hidden cost." Thanks to Susan's abuse of power, the staff was beginning to resent authority — any authority. This was not only polarizing, it was dangerous. Janet's concern was that if anyone in the group got promoted, they might get emotionally thrown overboard.

Once she realized this, Janet made a personal commitment not to engage in office gossip of any kind. She would listen to others with compassion, but she wasn't going to throw in her own war stories. Getting feedback from Angela helped Janet stick to this commitment under pressure.

Over time, this approach strengthened Janet's trust in herself, and the emotional tone Janet set by focusing on her work and staying out of the grapevine inspired further trust and the respect of her colleagues. The positive energy this created in her department didn't go unnoticed. Janet didn't know how long the situation with Susan would continue, but she just kept rowing. She worked to maintain a positive, group-oriented attitude and focused on effective actions that got necessary work done. Then, much to her surprise, she and everyone in the department were unexpectedly "rescued."

## Help Can Arrive Unexpectedly

The day started like any other workday. Janet had just finished greeting a team member in the parking lot and had poured her first cup of coffee.

That's when she saw the note from the chairman's assistant stuck to her computer screen. It read, "Janet, please come upstairs — Cynthia."

When the elevator doors opened on the floor of the executive suite, Cynthia met Janet with a warm smile and ushered her into an empty conference room. Minutes later, Keith, the CEO, swept into the room, came straight toward Janet, and shook her hand. "I just want to thank you for your hard work in the marketing division," Keith told her warmly. "I've heard wonderful things about you."

"Thank you, sir," Janet replied, puzzled. "May I ask what you've heard and who you've heard it from?"

"From Amy, one of the interns in your group," Keith replied.

Now Janet was really confused. Amy had been interning with her group for several months. Amy was respectful, hardworking, and quiet most of the time. How did the CEO end up getting feedback from an intern!?

"You look a little confused," Keith said, smiling. "Let me explain. Amy is the daughter of one of my close friends, Roger." Janet was stunned. Roger was the CEO of a prominent real estate development company in the area. "Roger and I play golf together," Keith continued, "and we talk through a lot of our challenges on the golf course. One of our challenges is that we both have daughters who want to be successful businesswomen. We both know we can't give our girls the type of experience they need in our own firms. So my daughter is interning at his firm, and Amy is interning with us. I do hope I can count on you to keep this confidential," Keith added.

Slightly shocked, Janet nodded.

"We'd been getting rumblings about some morale issues in the marketing department, so I have to confess I put Amy there to get her take on things. I told Amy straight up that I didn't expect her to be a mole, but her perspective on the situation would be helpful if she felt comfortable being candid with me."

"What did she tell you?" Janet asked him.

"She told me that, if it weren't for you, everyone worth keeping in that group would walk out," Keith said flatly. "She also told me Susan had gotten carried away with cost cutting to look good to our new CFO. Granted, my CFO, Don, can be a bear, but Susan overdid it and cut into essential resources. According to Amy, she was scapegoating junior staff members to cover up her own mistakes. I had Don go over Susan's expense accounts with a fine-tooth comb when I heard this because, in my experience, people who cover things up tend to do it in more than one area. Let's just say there were some mistakes there as well. Susan has been terminated."

"Wow," Janet said. "I had no idea. Amy is one of the most modest and humble people I've met."

"She'd better be," Keith replied grinning. "These kids have grown up with all sorts of advantages, so they have to work hard at supporting others to command genuine respect. I'm glad to hear she's blending in and working hard. You've made quite an impression on her as well. Amy tells me she wants to be the kind of leader you are when she's ready."

Janet was both flattered and relieved when she realized that, by mastering the Lifeboat lesson of staying mindful of how others felt about themselves in her presence, she had inspired Amy and protected her own career. That said, Janet told me she never could have imagined the way this challenge turned into an unexpected opportunity.

"I'm flattered, sir," Janet responded.

"I'm glad you feel flattered, but what I need to know is…do you feel ready?" Keith said, suddenly shifting into a more business-like tone.

"Ready for what?" Janet asked him.

"Ready to take over Susan's job," he told her. "We suddenly have an opening."

This is a true story, and I'll admit that I was very proud of Janet's happy ending. She deserved it. That said, even if the story hadn't worked out this way, the Lifeboat work that Janet did would have still been beneficial.

Having watched many clients courageously embrace their Lifeboat work, I've learned that whether they end up staying at their current firms, changing jobs, or even starting their own companies, they always manage to thrive. When you stay focused on the present, cultivate a positive attitude, and operate authentically with others, you attract people and opportunities that enhance your life and career.

# Lifeboat Question #8

# WHAT WILL BE MY STORY?

Over the years, the story of the *Titanic* has invited me to ponder not only what was unfolding between everyone involved,
but what it would have felt like to *be* one of them. When a great
story comes along, our imaginations often personalize the drama.
We compare and contrast events with our own life stories — and
this sense of connection feeds our understandings and our dreams.

Like any great story, the *Titanic* contains an unexpected plot
twist. The story starts as a party on the open seas and then — wham!
— it morphs into a primal struggle for survival. In countless ways,
this same unexpected plot twist can occur in our daily lives, and it
raises the same, urgent questions: Will the people on the lifeboats
reach safety? What must they do to survive? Will they make the
right choices? Each person's story will turn out differently based on
how they cope with that unexpected plot twist, which reflects their
unique strengths, struggles, mindset, and choices in that moment.

When it comes to your life story, deciding where you invest
your time and energy during the prime working years of your career

is one of the most important decisions you will ever make. It will dictate your level of financial security, the abundance you are able to create for yourself and those you love, and — most vitally — your sense of self.

Of course, as the *Titanic* shows us, there's no such thing as a perfect plan. Conditions can change swiftly, and when they do, your definition of success may need to change as well.

When Robert Hichens joined the crew of the *Titanic*, his goal was to follow orders and please his commanding officers by contributing to a stress-free journey for the passengers. Success, for Hichens, meant advancing his career: to get positive feedback, which might lead to another, even better job at a time when jobs in the shipping industry were scarce.

Margaret Brown's goal when she boarded the *Titanic* at Cherbourg, France, was to reach the bedside of her ailing grandson. In addition, Brown was part of the group of first-class passengers whose definition of success involved having a marvelous time and to be seen doing so!

After the *Titanic* hit the iceberg, circumstances abruptly changed, as did everyone's priorities. With survival uncertain, everyone had to adapt quickly and put aside whatever their story had been. Helping others and living to be rescued was all that mattered.

## The *Carpathia* Arrives

After seven long hours in the cold, dark waters of the Atlantic Ocean, the *Titanic* survivors on Lifeboat #6 were rescued by another ship, the *Carpathia*, in the early hours of Monday, April 15. The group had rowed together to keep warm, supported one another through physical exhaustion, and done their best to press through the trauma of watching the *Titanic* sink before their eyes. Their informal leader, Margaret Brown, had been keeping a watchful eye on Hichens, who was still mumbling under his breath about the dire consequences they faced.

Suddenly, one of the lifeboat passengers noticed a light on the horizon. Elated at the prospect of living to greet another day, a sense of tentative hope spread through the group.

There was more to this light than daybreak. The eagle eye of Frederick Fleet soon spotted two additional lights on the horizon. The group tried not to get overly excited because they couldn't be sure if they were looking at other lifeboats or not.

Within moments, Fleet confirmed a joyous discovery. The two lights on the horizon weren't separating; they were moving as one. This meant that they were looking at their long-awaited rescue ship — the *Carpathia* had been spotted!

In Logan Marshall's account, he quotes Margaret Brown's recollection of this moment, which is one of my favorite passages:

> Then, knowing we were safe at last, I looked about me. The most wonderful dawn I have ever seen came upon us.... First the gray, and then the flood of light.... For the first time, we saw where we were. Near us was open water, but on every side ice. Ice ten feet high was everywhere.... To the right and left and back and front were icebergs. Some of [the icebergs] were mountain high. The sea of ice was forty miles wide, they told me. We did not wait for the *Carpathia* to come to us, we rowed toward it.

According to survivor accounts, the view from Lifeboat #6 was awe-inspiring that morning. While their surroundings at daybreak sound terrifying, several of the survivors reported feeling virtually no fear by this point. Once aboard the *Carpathia*, many of them described a sense of being transformed by the realization of their individual significance in the scope of the universe. Their journey together had done more than preserve their physical lives — it had shifted their perspective about what life meant to them.

The captain of the *Carpathia*, Arthur Rostron, had experienced his own brush with destiny as he rushed through the Atlantic's treacherous ice field to respond to the *Titanic's* distress call.

Knowing that time was short and lives were at stake, Rostron took every practical precaution he could imagine, but he also pushed the limits. The *Carpathia* wasn't a transatlantic liner, and it wasn't built for speed. It was designed to reach a maximum pace of only 14 knots. Realizing they were in a race against time, Rostron posted extra lookouts to maneuver around the ice, turned off the ship's heating to ensure maximum steam for the engines, and roused all stokers to shovel coal into the ship's furnaces as fast as possible. After issuing these orders and explaining the risks to the crew, Rostron took a few moments for a signature gesture. Raising his right hand to his cap, he closed his eyes in prayer. After a shared moment of silence, everyone sprang into action.

Crew members later reported that the *Carpathia* strained and quaked as it reached 15, 16, and finally 17.5 knots racing through the dark waters of the Atlantic without radar. Thanks to the reflection from the stars, the lookouts were able to see the glistening icebergs as they whizzed past the ship. After miraculously dodging icebergs for roughly two hours, the *Carpathia* reached the distress position by dawn on the morning of April 15. For the next four and a half hours Rostron and his crew managed to reach all twenty of the *Titanic's* lifeboats and get 705 survivors onto the ship. When asked later how he managed to navigate this treacherous ice at such an astounding pace, Rostron replied, "I can only conclude that a hand other than mine was on the helm."

Arthur Rostron also exemplified the Lifeboat mindset under

pressure. Like Margaret Brown, he prioritized the well-being of others, displayed ingenuity in a crisis, and embodied a spirit of courage that united those around him to face the unknown and beat the odds. Not surprisingly, one of the most famous photos commemorating this rescue is of Margaret Brown presenting Arthur Rostron with a silver cup for his efforts the morning the *Titanic* survivors were rescued.

Getting out of the lifeboats and onto the *Carpathia* was challenging for the passengers, who were often physically shaking from the hours they had endured on the open seas. Some survivors sobbed and others buried their heads in blankets and laughed hysterically. Many of the people rescued stayed glued to the rails of the *Carpathia* looking for a sign, any sign, that more lifeboats might be found containing their loved ones.

For those anxiously scanning the vast ocean surrounding the *Carpathia*, the vista wasn't hopeful. According to the *Carpathia's* crew, roughly twenty-five icebergs estimated to be over two hundred feet high floated in the vicinity, plus dozens estimated to be roughly fifty to a hundred feet high.

Later that morning, around 8:30 AM, the *Californian* finally made it to the ice zone to take over the search for additional survivors. None were found. Shortly after the *Californian* arrived, the *Carpathia* left the area to ferry the survivors they had picked up to New York. It was time to get going. Some of the passengers were in urgent need of medical attention. During the three days it took for the *Carpathia* to reach New York, four additional people died and were buried at sea.

With the notable exception of Hichens, who remained estranged, the bond of unity among the passengers on Lifeboat #6 continued after they boarded the *Carpathia*. For many of them, the narrative that had defined their lives had been permanently changed. Haughty socialites had been reduced to shaking in tears for a cup of water. People from humble beginnings had summoned grace under pressure, faced death with confidence, and become informal leaders. We can't completely imagine the full impact of this experience on the lifeboat survivors — particularly those who had been rescued from this terrible ordeal only to learn that their loved ones were lost forever. However, what we do know is that the caring that was shared among the survivors was not organized along class lines. During the funeral service aboard the *Carpathia* to commemorate the over fifteen hundred people who had perished, socialites held the hands of passengers from steerage, and all embraced the simple truth that a life was a life. Many of the women were now widows, which united them in compassion. Regardless of one's social status, everyone recognized that all life was precious.

Then, as soon as word spread that the *Titanic* survivors were safely aboard the *Carpathia*, people around the world wanted to know the answers to the same questions we've been asking in this book: How did the *Titanic* sink? What went wrong? Could it have been prevented? What happened in the hearts and minds of people in the lifeboats? What inspired them to fight when all hope must have seemed lost? How did they survive when most people were untrained civilians facing terrifying conditions at sea? How did people maintain their composure and work collectively in such an extraordinary manner that night?

## Informal Leaders Emerge Under Pressure

As we've seen, and as eyewitness accounts testify, what made it possible for the survivors on Lifeboat #6 to beat the odds after *Titanic* sank was the emergence of an informal leader who fostered a spirit of inner and outer alignment within the group. By this I mean that the intentions, behavior, and values of the individuals, and of the group, became aligned in the service of their common goal — to survive. This attitude shifted the group's mindset from chaos and collective terror to a unified spirit of trust as they battled the elements together.

Every business that has become a household name and every song we find ourselves humming in the shower is born from a merger of talents. The group energy that amplified the individual strengths of every passenger on Lifeboat #6 works like the law of gravity, and it works for everyone.

This means it will work for you.

Attuning yourself to your body's deeper wisdom will take you from "what good looks like" to "what good feels like." Much like a tuning fork, once you capture a felt sense of "what good feels like" as an individual, your presence in a group can start a positive wave of group energy that can raise the resonance of everyone involved.

Margaret Brown illustrated this principle on Lifeboat #6. The attitude that infused her behavior started a positive wave of group energy that contributed to their survival. The individuals on this lifeboat became fully committed to supporting one another as equals and to pulling together in a spirit of mutual respect.

To thrive, we all need to work in an atmosphere where we feel valued — and emotionally safe. Yet this can be hard to find. In reality, many people report feeling stuck in companies where their energy is siphoned off into playing self-protective roles, and they don't feel they can realize their full professional potential. When this happens, we need to stop, remember the pitfalls of the Big Ship mindset, and make the Lifeboat shift. Once we operate authentically, our concept of self evolves, and we start realizing our potential no matter what our circumstances.

People who have made the Lifeboat shift cultivate the emotional agility necessary to adapt to changing circumstances. That's because, by learning to circumnavigate their inner icebergs, they are no longer stuck playing a part that has been scripted for them by others. When external conditions are in flux, and the definition of success morphs, they are better prepared to accept what's unfolding in the present and trust themselves under pressure.

Making the Lifeboat shift also helps keep us from making snap judgments about people. In most stories, it's easy to tell the "good guys" from the "bad guys," but real life is different. All people are capable of wise, caring choices, and of the opposite, and we can't always predict how we or others will respond in a crisis. The *Titanic* story makes that abundantly clear: When the stakes are highest, some people shift their mindset and rise to the occasion, and others become overwhelmed and stumble and fall.

Through learning to accept and trust themselves, people operating from the Lifeboat mindset cultivate the discernment necessary to make wise choices about when and why to trust others — particularly under pressure. As a result, the Lifeboat shift helps them internalize a powerful lesson from the *Titanic*: When fear is replaced by trust, self-help becomes us-help.

The eight questions posed throughout the Lifeboat Process are designed to help you clarify your own story and the narrative you are scripting for yourself. These questions invite you to pause, assess your options, and make well-considered choices in terms of where to invest your time and energy professionally. This involves asking: *Is the ship I'm on safe? Will it help me to operate authentically on my professional journey? Must I make the Lifeboat shift to save my career or help keep my firm afloat?*

And finally: *When is it time to ready the lifeboats and abandon this particular ship?*

## When It's Time to Abandon Ship

Obviously, the *Titanic* isn't always a perfect analogy for workplace issues. For instance, once the *Titanic* sank, everyone in a lifeboat was trapped until another Big Ship rescued them. In their careers, people are rarely trapped in their jobs in such a literal way. They have the option not just to make the Lifeboat shift in their attitudes and relationships, but to quit, row away, and find another company to work for.

When looking for a workplace where you can thrive, the size of the organization isn't what matters. It's the culture that counts. While the *Carpathia* wasn't as big a ship as the *Titanic*, it was still a large vessel, but Captain Rostron and his crew established a culture of communication that embodied the Lifeboat shift. They looked for warning signs, they planned ahead, and they pulled together under pressure to achieve their objectives. When it comes to your career, learning to get on the right boat involves learning to spot an organization that actualizes such values. When you do, row in their direction!

The Lifeboat Process shows us that, when it comes to our careers, we rescue ourselves — from the inside out. The truth is, we don't always have dramatic stories of being saved. In the real world, in corporate America, the challenges, problems, and obstacles never end. We will always need help to navigate treacherous professional waters and beat the odds. You know you've rescued yourself when the Lifeboat mindset defines your approach to every problem and relationship — that is, when you consistently make choices that align with your genuine values and create a positive atmosphere that supports others.

It's also helpful to bear in mind that unexpected challenges that require change don't always come in the form of disasters. Sometimes, it is an opportunity or a chance moment of good fortune that you never saw coming. That's why, for many people, it's advisable to start the Lifeboat work before deciding whether or not to leave their Big Ship. Every now and then, if you savor the small victories and keep rowing, an unexpected, dramatic turn of events rewards your efforts and you know, without doubt, that you've been rescued. As Janet experienced, trying to live authentically in every moment invites the kind of positive recognition that changes careers. After all, the passengers in Lifeboat #6 wouldn't have lived long enough to become "survivors" if they hadn't made the Lifeboat shift and stuck with it for as long as they needed to.

That said, an important question that remains for people struggling with job uncertainty is: When is it time to jump? When is that best? When do you decide that your company's Big Ship culture is too much to deal with, that things are a little too crazy?

As I note in chapter 3, evaluating whether your company is able to adapt to changing circumstances is critical to this choice. An obvious warning sign to watch for, one that impedes adaptability, is when everyone's behavior is designed to benefit the leadership team's personal interests.

But there are other signs. Big Ship thinkers often waste resources.

While people on the Big Ship may pay lip service to conserving resources, they tend to be more mindful of things that can be easily quantified and monetized. This makes sense in a climate that focuses on impression management because, if you can agree on how to measure resources, you can create spreadsheets and process plans that will make you look good and enhance your image.

Of course, as the *Titanic* story has shown, precious assets such as loyalty, motivation, and courage are tougher to quantify — and priceless.

Many clients tell me that, while they know they have to outsmart the competition to keep their firms in business, the harshest competition they face is often with their own coworkers. They report an "I've got mine!" attitude that seems to permeate their workplace and leave everyone ruthlessly focused on looking better than the next person to get their fair share of raises, bonuses, and promotions.

What's worse, many clients believe that this attitude stems from the top. When senior executives at these firms deliver public speeches about loyalty and the importance of people, while exhibiting a tendency to isolate themselves from the rank and file, they display a lack of alignment. Sure, the senior management team shows up for a photo opportunity on the factory floor. However, if a local line manager tries to have a thoughtful conversation about the firm's strategy with the top brass, the conversation often gets shut down quickly.

Are there hidden costs to ignoring warnings about dangers and proceeding as if it's business as usual? Just ask Captain Smith!

It's easy to point the finger of blame at others when our firms are underperforming and our careers are stalling — particularly if the people in charge of the organization aren't pillars of virtue. It's easy to see the faults of leaders, especially as resources are wasted, talent leaves, and poor decisions get rationalized.

But there are hidden costs for ourselves. The longer we remain with an organization that doesn't operate according to values that genuinely resonate with us, the more likely we are to mimic their values. The more we let fear of change or inertia justify staying in a bad job, the more fear and inertia can start to permeate our inner world. A sense of learned helplessness can take root, and it will take making the Lifeboat shift, along with the objective feedback and emotional support of people we respect and trust, to weed this out of our psyche.

How much is it worth staying in a job that is unfulfilling? What are the consequences in the rest of your life? I've seen clients who have developed a scarcity mentality — and the compulsion to fill an emotional hole with power and money, but this doesn't work. Without a sense of genuine meaning, a professional journey becomes a lonely ride.

So consider your feelings as warning signs. If adopting the Lifeboat mindset is not enough, and the only solution is to change your circumstances, then get in a lifeboat and go.

Ignoring the little signs of potential problems can have big consequences.

## LIFEBOAT CASE STUDY
### Tom's Shift Impacts Others

Tom, the head of a successful advisory consulting firm, still remembers the afternoon he realized it was time to make the Lifeboat shift.

"I was sitting alone at my desk reflecting on the hard work that my direct reports had put in over the course of the past year, and I was hoping to get two of them promoted and a bonus increase for the group. That said, I knew it was going to be an uphill battle with the chair of our compensation committee. We had just finished doing an interdepartmental feedback survey, and in spite of our group's value to the firm, the results hadn't come back in a manner that justified the compensation I felt many of them deserved."

Ironically, Tom's department was in charge of creating and administering feedback surveys for some of the firm's top clients. The irony of not being able to score highly enough on an internal survey to justify the compensation he felt his own team merited wasn't lost on him.

"When I stopped trying to overanalyze the situation and took the time to pause, I realized something vital for our group — and for our clients," Tom told me. "We all need feedback to remain competitive, but what we do with the information we collect depends on the attitude of senior management and whether the underlying tone that is driving the feedback process stems from courage or from fear."

Andy, Tom's CEO, was a Big Ship thinker extraordinaire. When compensation season rolled around, Andy routinely managed to get his chief human resources officer, Pete, to create a survey that justified the minimum compensation possible for the firm's employees. Andy and Pete always managed to take huge bonuses for themselves, of course.

As a result, Tom's team had lost some of their best employees, and Andy and Pete had ignored Tom's warnings about this. The previous year, thanks to Andy's denial about the need to take industry benchmarks into consideration when compensating top talent, one of Tom's superstar performers had jumped ship, and the firm subsequently lost an important client.

Andy and Pete's reaction was to blame Tom, who was told that if he lost another top performer, he would get a pink slip of his own!

As he stared at the compensation survey that rationalized giving his team the minimum possible bonus, Tom realized it was time to make the Lifeboat shift.

Because he was a feedback expert, Tom knew that a courageous approach to gathering information always stemmed from genuine curiosity about what was going on at all levels within an organization. While feedback might be funded by the top brass, its highest and best use was always to give people at all levels the opportunity to step back from their individual perspectives on challenging issues and consider the big picture more effectively.

This wasn't happening at Tom's firm.

That's when he realized it was time to stop trying to change the mindset of his current CEO and start looking for the positive actions he could take professionally. Tom started going through his contacts to see what made sense in terms of his next move.

His first opportunity came from Stacey, a former client who had worked with Tom on a large organizational feedback project that had turned out to be transformational for her firm's culture. They hadn't just loved Tom's analytics; they had loved the personal approach he took to helping members of the senior management team understand the importance of having personal conversations to ensure that key talent throughout their organization felt respected, validated, and heard.

"I can't promise you the kind of compensation you were getting running your former department," she told him over a business dinner. "But I can promise to have you on retainer for our firm. You taught us that conversations are every bit as important as the data we get from electronic surveys, and your approach to this has helped us increase retention in a way that's saving us a fortune. We need your perspective as our firm continues to grow."

While Tom's wife was supportive, they were both a little nervous about his reduced salary. Their son, Jason, had been having problems at work and had recently broken up with his girlfriend. It looked like he might be moving back in with them to get his own life on track.

Making the courageous decision to choose integrity over income, Tom and his wife decided that leaving his current position was a risk worth taking.

When Tom presented Andy with his letter of resignation, Andy's response was curt and professional. From Andy's perspective, Tom was a little too thoughtful and a little too high maintenance. Andy figured he and Pete could find a more junior person to manage the group for less money anyway.

Tom made sure that he put the Lifeboat values into practice when his new employer put him on retainer. He had frequent meetings with Stacey and the management team at her firm, and they engaged in frank and emotionally honest discussions about how to deal with challenging professional issues in a way that enhanced everyone's personal integrity rather than diminishing it.

In less than six months, Stacey's firm started working on a full-time position for Tom.

That's when Tom got an unexpected phone call from Jeff, the lead member of the board of directors at his former firm.

"Tom," Jeff told him bluntly, "it's a mess here and we need your help." Apparently, Andy and Pete had been implicated in some inappropriate behavior regarding their personal expenses, and they were both being replaced. "We'd like to hire you," Jeff told him.

"I…I'm sorry, Jeff. I'm on my own now, and I'm not available to come back to the firm," Tom replied, feeling flattered and flustered at the same time.

"We'd like to hire you to consult for us, Tom," Jeff told him. "Name your price — our reputation is on the block, and we need your help."

After considering all the offers in front of him, Tom made a different choice. Today, Tom is the CEO of his own consulting practice. He works with his former firm, with Stacey's team, and with clients around the world. His financial situation is great, and his professional satisfaction is even better.

That, however, is not the part of this Lifeboat shift that meant the most to Tom. It was how his personal journey ended up impacting his son.

Shortly after Tom left his dead-end position, Jason started reaching out to his dad for advice. Jason told Tom that he really respected his decision to live according to his values and that he wanted to be courageous enough to live that way himself. Over the course of the ensuing year, Jason managed to reunite with his girlfriend and get his career back on track.

A year later, Jason got married. At his wedding, Jason clinked his glass to make a toast to his father. "I'd like to thank my dad for being an example of the kind of man I always hope to be," Jason said, raising his glass to the room.

There wasn't a dry eye in the place.

When you make the Lifeboat shift, you don't just save yourself. That's because, when you live according to your values, you never know who's watching.

## LIFEBOAT CASE STUDY
### *Jose Learns the Power of Kindness*

Not long ago, I gave a keynote address to a group of market traders on the opening day of their off-site conference. I challenged the group to look for small moments in which they could do something unexpected and positive for someone else. Traders are a tough group. Ideas about random acts of kindness, paying it forward, and selfless altruism are not necessarily native to their thinking. But, to my surprise, my little exhortation worked. People shared contacts and useful bits of information. They sent one another complimentary texts. Small, thoughtful gifts were bestowed.

It was a start.

On the final morning of the conference, I stopped by the breakfast room before heading for the airport. As I was grabbing a bagel, Jose, one of the senior guys, approached me. "Maggie," he said, "could we spend a few minutes together?" He seemed somber. We settled into a quiet corner, and he launched into a personal story that I always think about when I start to lose faith in the power of "small-moment altruism."

"You know," he said, "as much as I liked your talk, I really didn't buy the stuff about looking for small moments to do something good for others." I said nothing. "I mean, it's so simple. I didn't see the importance of it in the context of my career." He paused. "But then I observed how much fun the other guys were having with the concept, so I decided to give it a try."

"What did you do?" I asked.

His facial expression changed. I was worried the little gesture had backfired somehow.

"I had flowers and a note delivered to my wife at home," Jose said.

Long silence. Once again, the tears! I found myself scrambling for the trusty packet of Kleenex I carry for those conversations when emotional honesty breaks through. Jose dabbed at his cheek.

"What was going on?" I asked.

"My wife was planning to file for divorce. She was going to take the kids and move away. Then she got the flowers and read my note."

"What did you write?"

"I just said I loved her. I was sorry I'd been away from home so much. I told her I couldn't do any of this without her. I planned to make things up to her and the kids as soon as I got back." His voice was thick with emotion. "A few minutes after she read the note, she called me."

"How'd it go?"

"We talked most of the night," he said. "I can't believe what I could have lost — this woman is the love of my life." He paused, then looked me in the eye.

"So I just wanted to say thank you. One little act of kindness may have saved our lives together."

Jose's story illustrates why simple acts of kindness are a big deal. You don't seek credit from others for what you do. They become part of the essence of who you are. You know what you have done. You are the witness of your altruism. That's what really matters.

Shifts like these form the foundation for every accomplishment you achieve when you adopt the Lifeboat mindset. You start navigating your own course in life and setting your own priorities. That's personal power from the inside out, and it gets reinforced every time you make a phone call to encourage a friend, tip a little extra, or help a stranger with directions even though you are in a hurry.

## Chart Your Own Course

As we train ourselves in little ways to remain aware of those around us, react helpfully when we can, and navigate life with a generous spirit, we are preparing ourselves for the big moments — whether we realize it or not.

Are you charting your own course professionally, or are you allowing others to write your script for you? What do you want your story to be? What brings out the best in you?

In our careers, our families, and our lives, the Lifeboat shift is about far more than simply avoiding danger. It's also about being in the flow of the possible so that, when the time is right, we have room in our own life stories for the waves of fate to guide us in astonishingly positive directions. When serendipity strikes, we often find ourselves on paths that elude the imaginations of Big Ship thinkers.

Sometimes our stories change when a new opportunity emerges. Sometimes a new person enters your life story and, through combining your strengths with theirs, an adventure unfolds.

The more agile you become at navigating the emotional turbulence that rocks your inner world, the more you'll attract the time and attention of others who have mastered these skills. This leads to the creation of professional alliances with colleagues who are genuinely supportive. Ultimately, they will share their strengths, contacts, and resources with you.

Here's the real power boost that making the Lifeboat shift brings to your career: Your goals and values will align with a larger vision of success that embraces both your individual fulfillment and the greater good of others.

Like all facets of the Lifeboat Process, this shift begins in your inner world.

Remember, there is always one person you can trust to help you tap into your strengths and muster the courage you need to lead — and ideally, be the person who can unite others as you decide together what the next positive step can be.

I believe that person is you.

# ACKNOWLEDGMENTS

E very book is a journey, and every journey changes us. The people who have shared the journey of creating this book with me have helped shape my coaching methodology, my approach to facing challenges, and the personal clarity I seek in my own life.

As always, I must begin by thanking my clients. We are all drawn to stories that help us navigate our own lives and careers more successfully, and those inspired by the real-life challenges of others resonate with what is most authentic in us all. While it's impossible to list all of the courageous people whose professional accomplishments have helped illuminate this work, let me simply say that I thank each and every one of you.

While there are those who witness our voyage, there are those in the lifeboat with us who help us keep rowing.

The journey from my initial inspiration to a successfully published book takes teamwork. I'm so delighted that I got the chance to work with the fabulous team at New World Library to bring this vision to life.

My heartfelt thanks go to my fabulous editor at New World Library, Jason Gardner. Jason and his colleague Jeff Campbell combined their talents to help this book realize its full promise. Their wit and wisdom helped me transform the timeless story of the *Titanic* into a strategic road map for professional advancement.

I'm also extremely grateful for the expertise of my agent, John Butman. John has been far more than an agent in this process. He has also been a mentor, a coach, and a trusted friend. Drawing on his vast reservoir of publishing experience, John has helped this book evolve. Throughout this process, John has also helped me grow in my ability to share what I've learned about professional transformation with enhanced clarity and impact.

When it comes to the writing process, I can't count the number of editorial conversations and draft revisions my husband, Charles, has gone through with me. Nor can I ever fully describe the inspiration I've gleaned from the special breaks we have taken together to keep fun, laughter, and love at the center of this process every step of the way. While all my books reflect the courage my clients have displayed as they face changing circumstances, this manuscript is also the reflection of a life that is shared with a devoted partner.

Special thanks also go to two of my dear friends who read this work in its infancy, Sabrina Chase and Carol Landi. One of life's greatest blessings is friendship. The intellectual generosity and passion for personal truth that inspired both of these amazing women to share their feedback with me early in this process is a gift I will always treasure.

When it comes to the blessings of friendship, there are many people in the business community, our local community, and the hometown where I grew up (Fort Worth, Texas) that merit special thanks. Much of this is due to the fact that my mother, Nancy Craddock, passed away in the midst of this book's creation. There are a multitude of people whose sheer kindness was a source of strength that helped Charles and me balance our coaching practice, the needs of our family, and my writing schedule during this challenging time. While I can't mention all these wonderful people, the following are some whose efforts have been central to our lives.

On the professional front, Charles and I would both like to thank our videographer, Andrew Smith. Andrew's talent and guidance have helped us illuminate this work through video and audio productions. Whether the task was overseeing multiple cameras at a keynote presentation or recording individual clips in his studio, he was there to help us balance our family's needs with our production schedule. Andrew is both a creative filmmaker and a fast friend.

We'd also like to thank Jayme Johnson, who has helped us with website design and social media messaging, as well as Carolyn Monaco, who helped us get focused in the early stages of our strategic planning for this book.

On a personal note, our deepest gratitude goes to Karen Niccolai and her staff from the Lakewood Village Retirement Community in Fort Worth, Texas. During my mother's final days, Karen cared for my mom in a spirit of love and devotion that can only be described as the answer to a prayer.

Charles and I would also like to extend our thanks to a very special group of friends and colleagues who were responsible for the types of synchronicities that kept us focused on our higher purpose under pressure. The unexpected signs from the universe that came to us through these inspirational people helped me stay centered until this manuscript was completed. Our lifeboat includes: Sharon Clarton, Valerie Hadley, Leslie Padilla, Amanda Pullinger, Eric and Terri Elliott, Roy Moore, Jerry Murphy, Rob Craddock, Fran Wilburn, and Steve Katten.

Whatever we accomplish in life, none of us do it alone. My hope is that this book will help others. Its completion reflects those who have helped me.

# ENDNOTES

## Introduction

p. 14   *Only about a third of the passengers and crew survived:* Among the many *Titanic* sources, there is no definitive count of total passengers and crew, nor of the numbers of dead. Wikipedia (https://en.wikipedia.org/wiki/RMS_Titanic) provides an accurate range, and I have mostly provided estimates.

## The *Titanic* Story: Big Hype, High Hubris

p. 21   *The RMS* Titanic, *created by a collaboration between the Harland:* Most details of the *Titanic* disaster in this chapter are from Logan Marshall, *The Sinking of the Titanic and Great Sea Disasters* (New York: L. T. Myers, 1912). However, I have separately cited other sources for specific details.

p. 21   *it had a total capacity for passengers and crew of 3,547:* The number of passengers is from both Titanicfacts.net and Wikipedia, "RMS *Titanic*," https://en.wikipedia.org/wiki/RMS_Titanic.

p. 23   *the seven steel cables anchoring the* New York *"snapped like twine":* Marshall, *Sinking of the Titanic,* 33.

p. 23    *April 12 and 13 were good days on the* Titanic: Marshall, *Sinking of the Titanic*, 35.

p. 23    *the ship's wireless room received a series of six warnings:* There is some debate about this number; some sources say that the final or sixth warning was not actually received.

p. 24    *From his position in the wheelhouse, Hichens would have been:* This description of Hichens in the wheelhouse is from Sally Nilsson, *The Man Who Sank Titanic* (Stroud, England: The History Press, 2011).

p. 26    *In his famous account of the sinking of the* Titanic, *Walter Lord:* Walter Lord, *A Night to Remember* (New York: Henry Holt and Company, 1955), 39.

p. 26    *Lifeboat #1 was lowered with only twelve occupants:* This detail is from Wikipedia, "RMS *Titanic*."

p. 27    *When Sir Cosmo's financial incentive to the crew members on Lifeboat #1:* Ken Rossignol, *Titanic 1912: The Original News Reporting of the Sinking of the Titanic* (The Privateer Clause Publishing Company, 2012), 129.

p. 27    *While this lifeboat had the capacity to hold sixty-five passengers:* This detail is from Wikipedia, "RMS *Titanic*."

p. 29    *some of the more prominent travelers were also given extra state-rooms:* Hugh Brewster, *Gilded Lives, Fatal Voyage: The Titanic's First-Class Passengers and Their World* (New York: Crown, 2012).

p. 29    *one female passenger from first class cried out, "Lifeboats!":* Don Lynch and Ken Marschall, *Titanic: An Illustrated History* (New York: Hyperion, 1995), 100.

p. 29    *While Hichens had served as a quartermaster on many vessels:* Lynch and Marschall, *Titanic*, 84.

p. 29    *Instead, Hichens froze at the helm of the lifeboat:* George Behe, *On Board RMS Titanic: Memories of the Maiden Voyage* (Stroud, England: The History Press, 2012), 371.

p. 30    *Brown helped her fellow passengers:* Marshall, *Sinking of the Titanic*, 119.

p. 30    *as did his fellow lifeboat passengers:* Marshall, *Sinking of the Titanic*, 118.

## Lifeboat Question #1: Is This Ship Safe?

p. 34    *The earliest roots of it have been traced back to:* Details and quotes from A. G. Hood, ed., *The Shipbuilder: The White Star Triple-Screw Atlantic Liners "Olympic" and "Titanic,"* vol. 6, (London: Shipbuilder Press, 1911).

p. 37    *His peers described him as "a bit of a chancer":* David M. Dore, dir., *Titanic Arrogance* (Surrey, England: Journeyman Pictures, 2011), http://journeyman.tv.

## Lifeboat Question #2: What Do I Do If I Sense Trouble?

p. 55    *Phillips was running on fumes at this point and responded:* Lynch and Marschall, *Titanic,* 83.

p. 57    *As luck would have it, just before Fleet spotted the iceberg:* See chapter 5 in Nilsson, *Man Who Sank Titanic.*

## Lifeboat Question #4: What If I Freeze in a Crisis?

p. 94    *he kept reciting a litany of discouraging facts, as if he was trying:* Marshall, *Sinking of the Titanic,* 118–19.

## Lifeboat Question #5: How Do I Find Inner Strength Under Pressure?

p. 113    *"Some of the passengers, in fact all of the women passengers":* Marshall, *Sinking of the Titanic,* 124.

p. 113    *it was the first ship Brown could book passage on to visit her sick grandson:* Brewster, *Gilded Lives,* 23.

## Lifeboat Question #6: Who Can I Trust in a Crisis?

p. 130    *Hichens made the mistake of referring to these unfortunate victims as "stiffs":* Marshall, *Sinking of the Titanic.*

p. 131    *"It's no use arguing with this man at all. It's best not to discuss matters with him":* Lynch and Marschall, *Titanic,* 144.

### Lifeboat Question #8: What Will Be My Story?

p. 173  *In Logan Marshall's account, he quotes Margaret Brown's recollection:* Marshall, *Sinking of the Titanic*, 124.

p. 174  *"I can only conclude that a hand other than mine was on the helm":* David Watts, "Spirituality at Work on *Titanic*," *Edmonton Journal*, April 14, 2012.

p. 175  *According to the* Carpathia's *crew:* This detail is from Wikipedia, "RMS *Titanic*."

# RESOURCES

The story of the *Titanic* in this book relies on all the following resources. Citations for specific details and quotes are in the endnotes. While there are many wonderful books devoted to different aspects of the *Titanic* story, the references chosen for *Lifeboat* focus on stories of individual passengers that help illustrate timeless lessons for dealing effectively with unexpected change.

## Books

Behe, George. *On Board RMS Titanic: Memories of the Maiden Voyage.* Stroud, England: The History Press, 2012.

———. *Voices from the Carpathia: Rescuing RMS Titanic.* Stroud, England: The History Press, 2015.

Brewster, Hugh. *Gilded Lives, Fatal Voyage: The Titanic's First-Class Passengers and Their World.* New York: Crown Publishers, 2012.

Lord, Walter. *A Night to Remember.* New York: Henry Holt and Company, 1955.

Lynch, Don, and Ken Marschall. *Titanic: An Illustrated History.* New York: Hyperion, 1995.

Marshall, Logan. *The Sinking of the Titanic and Great Sea Disasters.* New York: L. T. Myers, 1912.

Nilsson, Sally. *The Man Who Sank Titanic: The Troubled Life of Quartermaster Robert Hichens.* Stroud, England: The History Press, 2011. [Robert Hichens was Sally Nilsson's great-grandfather.]

Rossignol, Ken. *Titanic 1912: The Original News Reporting of the Sinking of the Titanic.* The Privateer Clause Publishing Company, 2012.

Watts, David. "Spirituality at Work on Titanic." *Edmonton Journal,* April 14, 2012.

### Documentary Film

Dore, David M., dir. *Titanic Arrogance.* Surrey, England: Journeyman Pictures (2011), http://journeyman.tv.

### Websites

Encyclopedia Titanica: http://encyclopedia-titanica.org

*Titanic* Facts: http://titanicfacts.net

Ultimate *Titanic*: http://ultimatetitanic.com

Wikipedia, "RMS *Titanic*": https://en.wikipedia.org/wiki/RMS_Titanic

# INDEX

# ABOUT THE AUTHOR

M aggie Craddock is an executive coach with over twenty years of experience working with clients. Best known for her work with Fortune 500 CEOs and senior management teams, Maggie has coached people at all levels of the professional spectrum. She has been featured on CNBC, ABC News, and National Public Radio and quoted in national publications including the *Wall Street Journal, Forbes,* and the *Chicago Tribune.*

Maggie is the author of *Power Genes: Understanding Your Power Persona — and How to Wield It at Work* (Harvard Business Review Press, 2011) and *The Authentic Career: Following the Path of Self-Discovery to Professional Fulfillment* (New World Library, 2004). She has also written a wide range of nationally syndicated articles on emotional agility in the workplace, and her methodology has been discussed in publications ranging from the *Harvard Business Review* to *O, The Oprah Magazine.* Maggie has been a popular keynote speaker at leadership conferences, executive education programs, university and industry networking associations, and personal growth seminars.

Before founding her executive coaching firm in 1998, Maggie worked as a lead portfolio manager for Scudder, Stevens & Clark. She received two Lipper Awards for top national fund performance: Best Short Term Multi-Market Income and Best World Income Fund over $1 billion in size.

Maggie received an MSc in economics from the London School of Economics, an MSW from New York University, and a BA in economics from Smith College. Maggie is also an Ackerman certified family therapist.

Maggie lives in Exton, Pennsylvania, with her husband, Charles Schneider. In her spare time, Maggie pursues her passionate interest in the great trees of the world. She and Charles travel across the country to learn about, photograph, and sketch trees in national forests and along nature trails.